Choc Wednesday Wisdom To Wake Your Soul

By Kimberly Ann Collins

Published By: SOAR (So Others Ascend Righteously)

Choose YOU! Wednesday Wisdom to Wake Your Soul
Copyright © 2017 by Kimberly Ann Collins - All rights reserved

Cover Design By: Sam Grisham
Layout By: Mike Simpson

PUBLISHER'S NOTE
This book was created in part from the author's life experiences.
Without limiting the rights under copyright reserved above, no part of this publication may be reproduced, stored in or introduced into a retrieval system, or transmitted, in any form, or by any means (electronic, mechanical, photocopying, recording, or otherwise), without the prior written permission of both the copyright owner and the above publisher of this book.
The scanning, uploading, and distribution of this book via the internet or via any other means without permission of the publisher is illegal and punishable by law. Please purchase only authorized electronic editions, and do not participate in or encourage electronic piracy of copyright materials. Your support of the author's rights is greatly appreciated.

Register of copyrights
Library of congress catalog card number

Printed in the United States

ISBN-13: 978-1545530061
ISBN-10: 1545530068

www.facebook.com/soar
www.twitter.com/dcsoar
www.instagram.com/dcsoar
www.dcsoar.com

DEDICATION

Dedicated to My Ancestors Who Whisper Wisdom in My Ears

CONTENTS

To Jannine

Thank you for
your Healing Balm

When you choose you,
you'll never lose

Kimberly
7/23/17

Choose YOU!

When Meredith Grey, a young intern on the television show *Grey's Anatomy*, asked Doctor McDreamy to choose her, my response: "choose you" kept ringing in my ear. Grey's request became more than just part of a script from an evening television show, but a memory and a longing heard sometimes within my own heart. What the actor conveyed were unspoken words left in unfulfilled hearts. Words most would not dare admit, let alone speak aloud. The positive; however, is when you are able to spin the words to empower yourself.

I am surrounded by some beautiful, bad, and bodacious sisters, but even they—like myself— sometimes wonder, "When is it my turn?" Wanting to be chosen by the perfect mate, perfect job; wanting their turn to receive a little help to make their load a little lighter. My girlfriend made me laugh at the irony of white women on soap operas who have no education, class, or money but manage to marry one rich white man after another. Their T.V. reality doesn't speak for even most white women.

The truth of the matter is there seems to be an imbalance of images and messages that are not funny or fair. It isn't fair that other sisters I know, like my friend Pam, have followed the path that was "supposed" to put them in a position to be chosen by the perfect mate or job, and they are still waiting to be chosen. My friend, like others, went to the "right" schools, put off having babies until marriage, and now the chances for children are becoming slimmer. She tells me with some laughter, she now believes her parents' recent generosity of huge sums of money is from the marriage fund they no longer think she will need.

1

Women are trained to be wives and mothers. If you are educated, that is a bonus. Becoming educated has its obstacles, most of which are within your control. You cannot control how others respond to you. My sister, Nikki, recently went for a job interview, and although she needed the job, she didn't like the energy within the environment. I reminded her that an interview goes two ways and that she needed to also choose them. I wanted her to know she has the power to choose. I know of sisters "hanging on" to three-party relationships, waiting for the man to choose, instead of them choosing not to participate in chaos. Just as there are some people holding on to a job waiting to be chosen for a promotion that serves only as a carrot to keep them working.

Personally, my heart plunged when McDreamy didn't pick Grey. It plummeted to memories of High School dances and later clubs—where I waited to be chosen to dance. It surfaced thoughts of rejection letters and other situations where I felt my happiness was dependent upon someone choosing me. I'm not sure when I started dancing alone at parties, but I did. It suddenly occurred to me that it was stupid not to dance because no one had chosen to take me to the floor. Slowly, but surely, this mentality started taking over other parts of my life. If there is a nice restaurant I want to try, I don't wait for someone to choose to take me —I take myself. If there is work I want to explore—I just do it, regardless of whether I become a millionaire or not. I am not waiting for someone to choose my idea or my talent. I choose me. I am not going to sit idle while someone tries to make up his mind about whether he wants to be with me. I want to be with me.

Choose you. When you choose you, you will not stay in relationships that do not honor your spirit. When you choose you, you will not harm your body with weight, alcohol, or drugs that will kill you. When you choose you, your choices are not predicated upon other's views or expectations, but what the Most High has moved you to do. When you choose you, you will not blame others for the space where you dwell. When you choose you, you "get it" when others choose to do something different. Choosing you is not selfish; it just means you do not come in body parts, and you must consider how adverse decisions affect the whole self. God knew this when you were "chosen" to be born and given the choice to breathe in life. Therefore, who are you not to choose you?

In *Choose YOU! Wednesday Wisdom to Wake Your Soul,* there are many Wisdoms similar to this introduction. This book is filled with Wednesday Wisdoms I have written over the past 15 years. The selections chosen are my best examples of wisdom gained while in the midst of battling life's humps and challenges. It also includes humorous anecdotes and exercises to assist you in accepting yourself as the expert of your experiences and your journey. As the expert, you are given space to claim and to write down your wisdom to revisit and to examine. Hence, I do not have the last say in what you decide to choose for you. You choose!

How to Use this Book

You will need a SOAR journal, or any journal of your choice, to complete these weekly exercises. There are 12 chapters (chapter 13 gives additional healing strategies) with no less than four Wisdoms per chapter, so you have a year's worth of work outlined for you to remember your wisdom and to write it down. Read one Wisdom a week, preferably on Wednesday, and complete the accompanying challenge.

You do not need to read the Wisdoms in order. In fact, if you are facing a particular challenge that is in a different chapter, feel free to visit that chapter. Most of the Personal Challenges and Writing Prompts are taken from SOAR's Writing for Healing Power Workshop series; therefore, its workability and success has been tried and tested. Each exercise will ask you to challenge yourself by replacing old thoughts with new ones and to compose a new poetry training wheel to write what you discover.

First, let me introduce you to SOAR's Poetry Training wheels. The object is not to make you a poet but to give you the words that evoke the same kind of tangible feelings any good poem or prose writing will evoke. The training wheels are simply your list of senses: sight, smell, taste, sound, and touch.

Below you will notice a sample list:

Sight	Smell	Taste	Sound	Touch
Bonsai Tree	Jasmine	Garlic	Wind chimes	Velvet
Apricot Sundown	Fresh cut grass	Lemon	Gun shots	Lint
Rolls Royce	Rotten eggs	Strawberry	Paper shredder	Tight curls
Twisted Steel	Onions	Chocolate syrup	Hummingbird	Baby's skin

After constructing your list, read the challenge and prompt. Use at least one word from each column to answer your challenge and to complete your writing prompt. To get started, try the following challenge and writing prompt, which is borrowed from Sam Grisham's poem, "My Come from Place" found in Chapter Two of this book:

Personal Challenge: Think about your "Come from Place," which is a culmination of experiences from childhood which impact your present. To help you, create a list of events which you still remember from your earliest experience(s) on earth. Do not compile them according to what you perceive as good or as bad, but focus on those memories that are more present and that you don't have to work hard to access because they always linger about in your consciousness. After you have bravely created a list of your experiences from your childhood to early adulthood, then use your writing training wheels to answer the following prompt. If the words I have chosen don't work for you, make a new list. You notice that I didn't just list a tree but a specific tree that has a specific shape and presence in the world. Whatever replacement you make, ensure it is specific, so that you can see, taste, smell, hear, or feel the emotions that surface for you in your writing. Think of the five senses as the clothes you put on your words.

Writing Prompt: My Come from Place….. You can either use this line once or repeat it as you access new emotions or experiences.

For example:
My Come from Place is full of **jasmine** scented dreams
Where **wind chimes** sing a melancholy melody of whispered affairs
Back alley deals leaving my mother's tongue sopped in **garlic** tears
My Come from Place, a space where I played Ring around the Rosie
Freeze tag, stop light, green light-childhood games

Rare as ghetto-laced **bonsai** trees
Where mommy and daddy's love played hide and seek in
My **tight curls** dancing about my head…..

Chapter 1

NEW YEAR: NEW YOU!

Surrender

After taking part in a pre-New Year's Eve spiritual fellowship and celebration, the word "surrender," given by Rev. Iyanla Vanzant, remained laced to my spirit and tongue. When I say "surrender," I really mean the action of spreading my arms wide and letting my head fall back as my eyes focus on the heavens. I mean the action of putting faith in the Creator that it will be as it is supposed to be without any interference from me.

Surrender is not about giving up, but it is about giving into a Creator who knows better than me. This knowledge does not make the action easier. As a parent, it is especially difficult to watch and to surrender the little girl I once knew to a world that might not love her as I do. As the little girl in me stomps out a path for herself, I do not give up on all I believe she can be and do in this world. I bow to the Creator on how she has designed my path. When looking at my own life, the things I've accomplished, and all the more I want to do, I must surrender to my faith that says the Creator has my back.

When I repeat my new mantra: "I surrender, I surrender, I surrender," I must remember not to look back. My cousin, Angie, said it best when she told me you gotta surrender and walk away. She said, "be like Forest Gump and run Kim, run." If I surrender, the doubt that I am not good enough or smart enough will dissipate and not resurface as a false truth. If I surrender, the false belief that I have control over the actions of others will release me from the outcome of what my words or actions put in motion. If I

9

surrender my fears, I must reinforce my faith so I don't walk backwards when a new challenge comes my way. I must also remember that fear and faith cannot be contained in the same space. I cannot believe in favor and look back to contemplate failure. There is no such thing as forward movement with a head turned backwards.

Look at the story of Lot's wife, who was immortalized as a pillar of salt because she could not surrender her past to focus on her present or future. There are steps to being able to surrender. The first step is to practice. You may want to start small like surrendering instead of honking at the person driving the car in front of you who slept at the green light. Instead of being wedded to being right, surrender the need to convince rather than offer another person your point of view. The ability to surrender is a learned behavior. As such, you might relapse into the old behavior. When the thought comes to your mind to not surrender, call that person who knows you, and who does not judge you, to talk you down and to bring you back to the peace that surrender offers. When you learn to surrender, you modify your behavior to learn a new state of being.

When you just "be," you are able to surrender to the harmony of life's breath. It is a cleansing breath, a freeing breath that lightens your load and the steps you take. There is a freedom that comes with not being tied to outcomes or trying to control stuff that is outside you. There is even a freedom when you let go of pushing and pulling for a particular thing to go your way, only to realize you have done all you can do, and the rest is up to God. I decided to surrender any feelings of guilt for things that I cannot change and to surrender relationships that do not honor the best of me. I acknowledge all the good and surrender all that is

10

antithetical to my wellness. I surrender myself to the power
of the healing breath that comes only when I truly surrender.

For this first week, I will offer the list composed in
the introduction ; however, feel free to replace the words with
your own. Read the challenge and prompt. Use at least one
word from each column to answer your challenge and to
complete your writing prompt.

Personal Challenge: Think about situations in your life that cause you stress. Is this stress a result of things you want to change or you want to control? Do you think a loved one will be better off if they just listened to your strategy or advice? Are you feeling anxiety because of a perceived outcome that you predict will result in failure? Meditate. Take seven deep breaths in, and release seven slow breaths. Do this three times. Surrender your breath in much the same way you need to surrender the need to be right. Once you have centered your mind, follow the prompt.

Sight	Smell	Taste	Sound	Touch
Bonsai Tree	Jasmine	Garlic	Wind chimes	Velvet
Apricot Sundown	Fresh cut grass	Lemon	Gun shots	Lint
Rolls Royce	Rotten eggs	Strawberry	Paper shredder	Tight curls
Twisted Steel	Onions	Chocolate syrup	Hummingbird	Baby's skin

Writing Prompt: In four lines or more, write I open my arms wide and surrender…

Make sure you put the clothes on your words to let you spirit touch, taste, hear, smell, and see your experience as you surrender. Post this writing on a mirror as a reminder, so when that partner or co-worker does something contrary to your expectations, or that child doesn't follow your advice, you remember to surrender because they are on their own journey too.

Get On Your Grind

I found myself sitting in a puddle of self- pity one day, ashamed that more of what I wanted and what I envisioned for myself had not manifested. My daughter asked me what was wrong. I told her I was stuck and that I should be doing more. She suggested I start conducting my SOAR retreats and other workshops. I had to admit that I had fallen off track while pursuing and completing my Masters. My daughter then pointed to some of my friends in the writing world who were doing their thing and asked me why I wasn't doing my poetry and putting my writing out into the world. I shrugged my shoulders. By this time, she had lost patience with me: "They are doing what they are doing because they are on their grind. Mommy, you need to get on your grind!" I blinked and wondered: "who was this child impersonating an adult and what does she know?"

Nothing will rock you out of a self-pitying stupor like your own child's voice. Her voice gets my attention because she knows me so well. Who else has had the privilege of knowing me from the inside out? To try and fool her is the same as trying to fool myself, only worse because she talks back loud enough for me to hear and is harder to ignore. It is as if she shook me from a coma. Her words reverberating over me, daring me to close my eyes to possibilities. I had to admit I shut some doors and dared not peak into others—too afraid that the task might be too daunting. There was also the thought that some doors were time sensitive and I just had waited too long.

My daughter's words jarred me because she forced me to face the fact that I was the only one locking the doors. Time was just an excuse to not move. I am surrounded by people who defy the constraints of time. I have a friend in his late 40s who feels after spending time in prison that he has just started living and is making the most of his time achieving literary goals. I have another friend who just became a grandmother and has decided to go back to school and to start a baking career. Neither he nor she is listening to time grind by while they go to work for what they want to achieve.

When you are on your grind, you don't have time to shop for excuses because you are too busy doing the work. The work feels harder when you feel like you are working, but it's not getting you what you want. It is frustrating trying to figure out what it will take to make that rejection letter turn into acceptance, or what new thing you need to do to revive your energy and imagination. I admit it is my impatience that brings my mobility to a grinding halt.

As I sit on the precipice of another year, I wonder if I am clear about what I want, or if I'm hiding in a time warp. My child's voice echoes in my ear, "if you are clear, then why don't you move?" It's at times like these that I know the Most High sees and hears my impatience and feels my inner battle to have the courage to listen and to move when the Most High says to move. I know the Most High gave me my daughter who is a light that shines so bright, I have to blink away from her glare. I shade my eyes from the shame of my daughter seeing me show up as less. She breathes new life into me to imagine new ways to be about the business of getting to the best of me by getting on my grind.

Personal Challenge: What are you not doing? What ideas come to you during your rapid eye movement (REM) sleep; that time when you are almost awake and your ideas and thoughts are in full motion? Write those ideas down even if they appear crazy and extreme, and then think about the steps

Sight	Smell	Taste	Sound	Touch

needed to fulfill your ideas. This is the life you dream for yourself. Dare to dream and to do.

Writing Prompt: I dare me to…. The sky is the limit and so are lines you will write of all you dare to do and to be!

Process the Moments

Coming into the New Year, the idea of process has been part of my conversations. For instance, my friend, Liana, asked me whether my efforts to get published met my expectation, which means I might want to look at my process. A new friend shared with me her process of ending a long-term relationship held together only by the habit of years. Then there is the sister-writer who asked me, of all people, how to keep writing when her work is rejected. Whether the subject was love, school, ambition, or even writing, the question became how to figure out and how to honor the process to gain the desired outcome. The first step must begin with changing the thought process of what you conceive and what you believe you are able to achieve.

From the moment you are born to the day you die, every moment of your life gives into a process to experience an even greater moment. There is a process, when you are a baby, you must experience before you walk or talk. There is a process to experience before that moment when you finally tie your shoe or read a book by yourself. There is also a process to unlearn how to smoke, eat, or drink too much. In some cases, you have to unlearn how to love someone who is no longer good for you. No one just falls in love, and no one just falls out of love; there is a process. Regardless of how the relationship ends, there is a process you experience to learn and to heal from the lesson. Belittling the self or letting others say you are crazy for still loving someone does not hurry the process; it just makes you feel bad during the process. Healing is a process you must honor and one that only happens once you dismantle the fear.

Procrastination, masked as process, is only a longer word for fear. If you are stalling about letting someone out of your life, you must make sure it isn't the fear of being alone keeping you there. If you are blocked from writing or sending out that next poem, essay, or great novel, you must ask yourself is it the fear of it not being good enough that makes you pause on the send button or holds your pen in mid-air. Sometimes procrastination is part of the process. You may need to clean up the house, straighten the work area, and sharpen the pencils before you begin the work. You may even need to allow yourself a time limit to cry and to call him or her in order to wean yourself away from the relationship. Whatever the process, you must know the difference between procrastination and process. Procrastination is only part of the process if the lessons are learned, if the tasks are completed, and if you are able to get to your next best moment.

You can look at life as a process of moments. The only way to enjoy the moment when your book is published is to continue to write without giving a damn what anybody thinks. The only way to enjoy a life free of habits that do not honor your temple is for you to go through the process of self-discovery and recovery. In order for you to get the love you deserve, you must go through the process of healing and learning what you need versus what you want. In order to honor your process, you must first know your process. Knowing your process means you must not only be patient with your process but also bump up your faith in the process of claiming the storehouse of good waiting on you.

Personal Challenge: What is on your things-to-do list for you? Have you written that personal statement for a college application? Is your job search stalled? Do you need to put together an action plan to change your living situation? Name the thing, and list five action steps. Make them small things like writing the first paragraph of your personal statement. Do not overwhelm yourself with a task. Once you have completed your list, follow the writing prompt below.

Sight	Smell	Taste	Sound	Touch

Writing Prompt: For this exercise, the focus is not on the procrastination but on the process and its outcome. You can begin with My process is… or I have faith in the process to…. Once your poem is completed, you will realize how you get in your own way and how to be well on your way to achieving your goals because you just completed the first step of your process, which is to just do it.

Wide Awake

One day into the New Year, and my friend Collette exclaimed how this year is going to be better because last year was so bad. Well, what was so bad about last year? I asked her. She said she broke up with her fiancé and, as a result, she faced a lot of emotional turmoil. I told her, she bet not tell another soul that lie.

It was a lie because if she had walked down that aisle, she would have walked into a fiery furnace of woe. The first woe is that she knew beforehand that her spirit was in jeopardy. She was feeling like parts of her were being syphoned and were part of a bargain of which she was not in agreement. She was lying to herself in order to not rock the proverbial boat. She was lying because she loved this man, saw the good in him and thought part of love was sacrifice, but then she woke up.

She woke up and saw pieces of herself scattered around a house he reminded her was not hers. She woke up to the self that had crawled into a corner waiting for the storm to blow, so she could once again recognize the lover who curled her in his arms at night. She woke up and realized her past experiences already prepared her to see what was in front of her and the hollow and unforgiving silence it leaves inside. Her spirit slapped her awake to save itself from an imminent death and departure from self.

Waking up is not a bad thing. Of course that means she has to stare down her own truths, drink a tall glass of integrity, and swallow it without letting any of it drip out the sides of her mouth. I shared with her that I, too, woke up last year. I woke up to how not living in my own integrity affected who I decided to love and what I was willing to take

19

in order to be in a relationship. I was not in the "right" relationship with myself. I was not living within my integrity. I was asleep inside a belief system which told me men don't stay. I knew how to get over their departure because that is what I practiced. The truth is having someone commit and stay was not a practiced muscle, so I choose men with exit signs over their heads. I woke up and realized I was not living within my integrity.

Being suddenly awakened while snuggled under covers is like being pimped-smacked wide awake with me as the only person to smack back. Once awake, it is impossible to return to a dream that has become a nightmare. The covers no longer offer warmth. I can no longer participate in relationships that do not honor me no matter how parched I might be. So I told my friend, last year was a great year because she woke up, and once you wake up, you cannot go back to sleep.

Personal Challenge: What are you sleeping on? How have you slept on your relationship with yourself or in other areas of your life? Take a minute to sit with this idea, and then write it out in the affirmative following the prompt.

Sight	Smell	Taste	Sound	Touch

Writing Prompt: I woke up and… Once you rubbed the sleep out of your eyes and removed the crust from your spirit, what did you see? All of what you see will not look or feel good. What will feel good is seeing honestly where you need to go and where you want to be. What will feel good is being alert enough to not be a Rip Van Winkle and let another year go by with you still being asleep, so put the clothes on the words to make sure you stay wide awake.

Checkin' the List

I did something recently that I have not done in a long time. I read some of my old diaries. It was a New Year tradition for me to look back over the previous years to chart my progress. I abandoned the tradition after I revisited some episodes I wanted to remain forgotten. However, on this day, I was in need of some clarification and some direction that could only come from the candor spoken in the pages of my past. Those pages revealed similar crossroads at different points of my journey where I felt uncertain and frustrated with my progress. I was amazed at how the same stuff kept coming up decade after decade. I was even more amazed that I used the same strategy each time to calm the fears and to lessen the anxiety. Whenever I felt my progress blocked, I would make a list of things I needed to accomplish to remove what I saw as the obstacles in my path. A list was needed to clarify my focus and to chart my course. The problem was not with the list; the problem was not giving enough credit to myself for what I accomplished on my list.

Each year, I checked the lists and checked them twice to see where I needed to go. I paused at times in surprise at how far I had come—only long enough to push the bar up a little higher. I have a fear of complacency, so I keep looking around for more that I need to do to get where I believe I want to be. So I created a new list without taking a breath of satisfaction. I didn't breathe long enough to really celebrate the single mother who moved herself from welfare to work. I didn't stop long enough to inhale the satisfaction of being able to finally get braces, buy my dream car, pay off school loans, buy a house, and finally graduate from college and grad school. I just crossed these things off my list as I created new lists. I checked off the lists without really celebrating the accomplishments on my lists. I've come a long way from that single mom on welfare, so why not celebrate her? Finishing undergrad after 20 years was a real thing that, in turn, inspired other friends and family members to return to school, so why not really celebrate that?

Don't get me wrong; anybody that knows me knows that a party doesn't owe me a thing, and I have celebrated me. I have been remiss in dismissing the extraordinary as ordinary. Each thing leads to the next thing, so no one thing really can be rated as larger than the other. Life is a series of steps. These lists saved me when the dark spaces wanted to swallow me whole. These lists were simple prayers that were not overlooked by God but by me when my cinema-influenced imagination did not match my present-day reality. Perhaps, I am supposed to be exactly where I am? Perhaps, my audience is not to be larger than my listserv or my classroom? Perhaps, being able to celebrate my blessings regardless of the size of the stage is me showing up in the full regalia of my blessings? If I truly believe that I am earning my space on earth, should I question the pace or learn to celebrate the process?

When I forget all that I have accomplished, I do a disservice to my journey. I am who I am because of all the muck and all the joy I have walked, danced, skipped, and sometimes run through. Lists are important to keep me on task and to mark my journey, but I gotta check once to see how far I've come and check it twice to make sure I celebrate it all.

Personal Challenge: Compose a list of your accomplishments. If you have a previous goals list, consult it and check off your completed goals. If not, compile a list of goals you know you've completed in the last five years that you have not acknowledged. Also, make a list of 10 goals for the next five years and 10 years. A goal can be as simple as filling out a college or job application to buying a new car or house.

Sight	Smell	Taste	Sound	Touch

Writing Prompt: After consulting your list, in seven lines, or more, compose an affirmation of celebration. I celebrate me….. Repeat this phrase before writing each new goal reached, and even include a celebration for the goals you will complete in the next five or 10 years. Once completed, post in a visible location in your home or office.

Chapter 2

MY COME FROM PLACE

My Come from Place

my come from place is scary
bittersweet
long on memories and high notes
my come from place hunts night like coon smell
hound dogs anticipating the kill
shine wet, air suck nostrils, flared
a heart thump, tail wag vision of the beast mirrored
in the dark tunnel eyeballs.

raped (get up BobbyJo)
on a bare wood floor (I'm gon' tell I swear I'm gon'
tell)
in the summertime (did he touch you?)
at grandma's house (did he touch you down there?)
grit red tongue sponge in my mouth (stop please
stop)
snuff juice stink running down my back (you better
not tell girl)
stole (get up BobbyJo)
like me.

twenty-one ain't no fun cause every deuce is wild
one-eye jacks and jokers stack the game for every
child

my come from place is scary
bittersweet
long on memories and high notes

my come from place where Vanessa robbed a bank
and kissed a guard
stole his balls through iron bars
laughed at his manhood on the six o'clock news
and I said she didn't do it
we played marbles and mudpies
traded ponytails and cat-eyes
but the judge said Life
now give his balls back

my come from place

where Big Red was a woman who married a man
who left her for a man who loved men
who called my mother sister and my cousin son
where Lucinda's house was rank with bootleg
whiskey and Wild Irish wine
and baby sister's sweet honesty was manufactured
by Avon
and when the brass knob turns, run. you better run
or be prepared to see "girl, lemme tell you how
good your mama was …
she didn't lay all her tricks 'cause she could play her
tricks"
put your hand in the black
do you ever get it back?

jump back sally jump back

where JohnDog's belly ballooned from codeine and
cocaine and co-living with all that dying
and all the furniture wears a price tag
where Goofie shot his best friend for a mixed bag
and T's and Blues and Oxy-tudes date the ladies of
all-day and every day is festival
see the man with the white balloon
he will take you there

my come from place is scary.
bittersweet.
long on memories and high notes.

my come from place
nestled snug amid thick green scented pines
shaded cool by healthy overgrown oaks
courting the shell white sands of a living lake
flirting with a universe

my come from place
where mama didn't say be good
just

be careful

-Sam Grisham

29

Personal Challenge: This exercise is how most SOAR workshops begin. It is one of the cathartic and revealing of all the exercises because it forces you to visit places that are sometimes dark and scary and act as clouds hovering over your ways of being. Find a quiet safe space for the writing. Do not edit the experiences that come up for you. Just write them down. Chronological order is good but not necessary because you will see as you begin to access memories how they will begin to link themselves to one another. Do not compile these memories according to what you perceive as good or as bad. After you have bravely created a list of your experiences from your childhood to early adulthood, then use your writing training wheels to answer the following prompt. Remember to put clothes on your words so you will see and feel the texture of their meaning. After constructing your list and reading Sam Grisham's poem, "My Come from Place," answer the challenge.

Sight	Smell	Taste	Sound	Touch

Writing Prompt: My Come from Place….. You can either use this line once or repeat it as you access new emotions or experiences.

Starting from Nothing

When I was first introduced to this idea of "starting from nothing" in the Landmark Forum, I didn't know what the heck they were talking about. I mean, I am a composite of all things experienced and lived. I am my hopes, dreams, and desires. Even as I am writing, there is a part of me that is outside of myself wondering what words will come next. I must tell you, it is exhilarating! Last week, I was terminated from a job which confirmed the work SOAR will do to rebuild our village one circle at a time by providing writing for healing tools and mentors to young black women who are 17–25 years of age. I am presently waiting for the renewal of my teaching contract to arrive in my inbox, and I am set to go on an interview tomorrow to check out another employment opportunity. If that is not enough, I am relaunching my business, SOAR, as a non-profit. Next week, I will have my first Board meeting. So when my father called me recently and asked me how things were going, and I told him everything is up in the air: my job, my business, my house renovation, my finances; he thought he should call back another day. I told him he didn't need to because I was not depressed or discouraged. Everything is perfect.

There is a certain wonder, a kind of Christmas morning excitement in not knowing. I knew early on this year that a change was coming. I did not know in what form, but I felt it. I feel like I've been on the edge of my seat in a movie theater watching my life without any popcorn. The first shift occurred at the beginning of last year when my daughter told me not to think about entering another degree program because I already had everything I needed; I needed to just go do the work. Taking her advice, I went to the powers-that-be at my university and piloted SOAR's My Daughter's Power Circle. Those young college women who participate in the Power Circle inspired me to get back into my game. They reminded me that I am supposed to do much more than provide English instruction, grade papers, and lecture classes. I had no way of knowing how those young women would respond to that circle, who would come, or who would remain both semesters. The group started at a staggering 20, and by the end of the second semester there were 10, and six made it to the closing dinner. The numbers were not as important as what they gained. One of them shared that she learned "women are not my competition." That is huge! Most shared they didn't know they could find strength and non judgement amongst women they did not know. Although, I still enjoy teaching, I feel my focus begin to lean in another direction.

I am like my house that currently is without a kitchen and working bathrooms; in a state of renovation. It has been over a year since the architect abandoned the project leaving my home in chaos and me without the funds to complete it. I have been blessed with dollars to hire essential folks one by one to do their part. It is a slow process, and one that has tested my faith and caused me to beat up on myself for bad decisions and for not being smarter. All the negative old tapes ran rackets on my brain. None of which made me feel good and none of which helped me to get the job done. It was not until I adjusted my internal thoughts and talk that my power returned. I regained power once I decided to really look for what I needed to learn.

I learned I need to trust myself. I could say I wasted a lot of money learning this one lesson, but that would only be true if I didn't get the lesson. Recently, I was telling someone how I was waiting for an agent to publish this book of *Wednesday Wisdom: Words to Wake the Soul* and my book of poetry, *Bessie's Resurrection.* I told her all the reasons I didn't want to do it because of my first experience with self-publishing. This woman, who I had just met, went straight to the marrow of me and said "you need to control your shit." Well, if I had some pearls on, I woulda clutched them. Her words were my "AHA" moment. Me, my house, and my books are all at the same point of nothing, therefore; the possibility of becoming more is inevitable.

Personal Challenge: Look at those spaces in your life that appear askew and out of place. Places and spaces that are imperfect. If you understand the notion of starting from nothing, you will realize everything is as it should be, and it is perfect. It is perfect because it is the beginning of a new way of being or creating in the world. Shun those ideas of perfection and claim it as already perfect.

Sight	Smell	Taste	Sound	Touch

Writing Prompt: It…… is perfect and so am I or All things are working together for my good…

Sula

I have lost count of the many times I have read Toni Morrison's *Sula*. It is a book that nurtures my feelings about sisterhood and continues to nourish what I know about the importance of a woman feeling whole unto herself for herself.

When Sula comes back to her small Ohio hometown from the "big city" without the hindrance of children or a husband, she is regarded as strange and as a woman to fear. Her grandmother asks: "when you gonna settle down and have some children?" Sula replies: "I don't wanna make nobody else. I wanna make myself." My soul jumped at this line in my twenties and continues to do flips in my fifties when I read this line. It has always been important to me to experience the world on my own terms.

I knew in my twenties that I wanted to be married and to have children, but it was more important for me to have me first. Therefore, I decided I didn't want to have a child until I was 30 because by that time I would have traveled the world and would be ready to share myself with someone else. I did travel, and I did have a good time in the world unencumbered by children. I remember men being surprised that at 29 I did not have a child. So when I did have my daughter at 30, I was ready. I was ready to share all of what I love about being a woman with this girl-child I birthed. I was excited to share all that I learned about being a sister to other sisters with this little sister who was now the center of my world. I was in love with the possibility of showing her the world. I could do that because, like Sula, I took time out to make me first.

Sula matters to me because she fostered the growth of my womanist sensibilities. Sula was raised in a household governed by women. It was rumored that her grandmother, Eva, had cut off her leg to get insurance money to feed her kids and to buy them a home after being abandoned by her husband. She was a matriarch who was never without the company of men who sought her wise council, wit, and ability to play a mean game of checkers. Sula's mother, Hannah, was a woman who deeply loved Sula's father and in order to survive after his death, she took pleasure from other women's husbands. Hannah believed everybody needed a little touching and holding each day. Although, she never had many women friends, the women folk didn't mind her because she made their men feel so special when she called them "suga" and shared a little of her "suga" with them as well. Unlike Hannah, the women folk in the town did not like the cavalier way Sula had sex with their husbands and discarded them without any pleasantries. The women talked about Sula and so did the scorned men. She experimented with men in much the same way a child does with a new toy and throws it away after it has lost its charm. When she experiments with her best friend Nel's husband, it challenges their relationship. Another favorite line is when Sula tells Nel, "I didn't take him. I just fucked him." Here is the test of sisterhood that always creates profound and divisive discussion in my freshman English classes.

I wrote a poem about my mother once in which I state that she is the one who taught me about sisterhood. I remember crying because my good friend had slept with my boyfriend, and my mother cautioned me to not let something that I wasn't going to do anyway to disrupt our friendship. Later, it dawned on me this friend had other issues, and sleeping with my boyfriend wasn't about me. Nel comes to this same realization after Sula dies when she cries, "oh Sula, we was girls together." Knowing the importance of sisterhood is a vital part of any woman's maturation. Sula was unconventional. I am not Sula, but I admire all of the women who help make her and who help make me. I also admire that she had the guts to live life on her terms and to see life as an experimental thing that if taken too seriously will be missed.

Personal Challenge: The people we come from impact our way of being. Think about how those who nurtured you or who did not nurture you shape your decisions and movements. Remember, there is not good or bad; it is only who they are and who you have become. A look into these personality shapers helps you to begin to sift out what actions you independently take and those that are in response to a learned ideal.

Sight	Smell	Taste	Sound	Touch

Writing Prompt: The People I come from.... In this poem you will describe their beliefs, actions (which maybe antithetical to their beliefs) and physicality. After writing this poem, stretch yourself to write another poem: I am becoming.....

The Butterfly

My cousin, Terrence, told me a story about a butterfly who was helped out of its cocoon too early. It was helped by a caring individual who saw how hard the butterfly was struggling to break free of the cocoon. Once the butterfly was helped, his wings were not strong enough to fly. See, the butterfly needed the struggle in order to strengthen its wings. This story is applicable to many situations we encounter in life.

I am guilty of helping the butterfly. I see a loved one in need and step in to assist, believing I have just the remedy they need. I believe I am able to fix a problem that is not mine or alter a life story I did not write. What I see as my well intentioned intervention is really my intervening on that person's necessary life lessons—the life lessons the loved one needs to build the muscle and wit necessary to push forward or to climb out of the pit where he or she may fall as one learns to fly.

It is hard to watch a loved one burst seams as they struggle out of an abyss of childhood nightmares to fit into this thing called life. It is equally hard when it is a love one you birthed or one you know is full of potential if only he or she will seize the positive instead of the negative notions fluttering about his or her head. There is always a sad story to tell; ask any celebrity who triumphs over adversity who later bares their soul. The difference between the celebrity with a sad story of strife and struggle and regular folk is air time. The point of their story is how they struggle out of the cocoon filled with nightmares of abuse, neglect, and self-hatred to eventually break free with beautiful wings that are able to fly.

In my own attempt to help the people I love, I have found that my well intentions are what they begin to struggle against. I have learned it is not my job to save anyone. I can act as a support when asked, but I must not be wedded to the outcome, and I must be able to step aside when I realize this is a struggle they must endure alone. Life lessons are an individual thing taken in a classroom filled with other people trying to get their own flying lessons. The classroom is full of people trying to earn and to strengthen their wings the only way they can, on their own. As a loving bystander, all that is left to do is to pray your love one finds and retains the strength to fly on purpose.

Personal Challenge: Who are you trying to fix? If you can understand that people aren't broken, then your need to fix them will be halted. If you realize that we are all made up of a composite of tapes that began recording our actions, responses and experiences from our birth, then you will realize you lack the ability to change what you did not create. To better understand the old tapes they may rewind in their head that keeps them from moving forward or from giving a different response, first access the old tapes that make you believe it is your job to fix someone else. What tape keeps rewinding in your head to make you believe you are responsible for someone else's wellness? How does fixing someone else feed or empower you? Are your actions motivated by ego? Rewind your inner tape that has recorded experiences which say to you this is your job and responsibility and if you don't do it, you will be unhappy.

Answer in the prompt below.

Sight	Smell	Taste	Sound	Touch

Writing Prompt: When I listen to what's on my inner tape recorder, I hear?

Chapter 3

WHO AM I?

Living Courageously

Flying under the radar of life is unacceptable. You are cheating yourself and the universe from your ability to earn your space while you are here. It is so easy to say what you can't do because you are really just scared to do. The fear comes from not knowing or not believing that your talent is big enough for the world. Recently, I assigned my freshman students with the task of writing a two-page essay to answer the question: "if money were not an issue, what work would you do for free to earn your space on earth?" Before they found themselves in a job they hated, confined by responsibilities, hemmed in by bills, or spinning their wheels trying to find the best get rich scheme, I wanted them to first tap into their well of abilities and talents as their guiding force. I wanted them to have a blueprint of their true desires and a vision of themselves that understands the part they are to play in the universe.

One of my students, who had a wonderful vision of herself as a photographer, ended her essay by stating she would shun that career to play it safe and to become an accountant. Playing it safe is something children do to impersonate grown-ups who decide dreams are fairytales because one too many disappointments broke their courage to dream again. Children watch their parents "playing it safe" by going to a job they hate instead of giving that "thing" another chance. After reading her essay, I wondered did she know about James Van Der Zee or Gordon Parks, Black men who left lasting images of Black life. Money was not their motivation; it was their ability to interpret life through the lens and to give it back to a people who were not used to seeing themselves that provided the fuel for their ambition.

If they played it safe, a visual memory of a people would not exist.

Playing it safe has the ability to impact all aspects of your life, even how you choose to love. Walking love's precipice is as risky as stepping out on a dream you have of yourself. You have a dream of what you look like as a success in the job you love just as you do of when you are in love. Both journeys are a calculated risk. Sometimes you choose to "retire" from love's reach because of too many false starts which leaves your spirit feeling and looking like a wilted plant unable to be revived by water or sunlight. You are resigned to believe "maybe next life-time" it will happen for you. Yet, you know it's possible because there are couples who have lasted 50 years, and couples who wait on love almost 50 years. I know of one such story of a woman who found her soul mate in her late 40s. She was the wife for whom her husband had prayed. They were in sync. Anyone who ever had the opportunity to be around them could just see the mutual care, respect, and love they had for one another. After five years of marriage, she suddenly died. He was devastated, but he was comforted in knowing that they had done 50 years of lovin' in five years because they loved courageously.

It is not the time you are given; it's what you do with time. Now is the time for you to tap into your passion to earn your space. Do not waste time crawling in a shell to hide from your talent and ability to love. Life is not for the faint of heart or for the wilting violets. You must have courage to push back fear and to access the faith that allows you to answer affirmatively that you did more, rather than less, with the life God so graciously gave you.
Live it courageously!

Personal Challenge: Similar to what was asked of the students, think of the thing you would do for free. What is the dream that you have always had for yourself but thought it was impossible? Trace your dreams from childhood. When we are children, we have an abundance of wishes and dreams we really believe are able to come true. Look into that treasure chest of dreams and pick one to make a reality.

Sight	Smell	Taste	Sound	Touch

Writing Prompt: In my treasure chest of dreams and wishes I have…..

Attitudes Talk

For my Graduate School essay exam, I had to ponder the question of whether "attitudes are everything." I thought about how you can see peoples' attitudes walking up a street. I thought about how you can sometimes tell what you're going to meet by the twist or dip of the walk. I thought about how attitudes show in eyes that sparkle with kindness, or roll in projected disgust or disinterest. Attitudes ride on smiles, glide on grins, or move you away with sullen pouts. More often than not, you meet a person's attitude before they've even had a chance to speak.

Have you ever looked at a person and wondered if they were having a bad day and then see them again looking the same way? Have you ever noticed someone, regardless of the kind of day they're having, who can always give you a smile?

Life offers a mixed bag of good and bad things that will occur. It does not happen to just you, but to everyone. It is how you choose to respond to these events that makes the difference. There is an old saying: "some people take lemons and make lemonade," and you can add that some people make lemon juice. The lemonade represents a sweet, refreshing drink, an attitude that refuses to live life without sugar. For those who can't find the sugar in life, their attitudes become like lips distorted by the bitter taste of the lemon. These are the people whose attitudes are mired in the muck of what life did not give them, with their dreams soaked in sorrow.

It really is all about your attitude and how you choose to view situations in your life. If you have the attitude that nothing good happens, then you doubt your joy and are unable to fully embrace it. You are always looking for the other shoe to drop, to prove happiness is not real or that it doesn't last long. Without knowing it, you are manifesting your fears, negating your faith because the two don't co-exist. Without knowing it, you are giving unforeseeable power to unknown entities that projected this belief on your life. Without knowing it, you are letting situations and outcomes of the past alter your attitude about the future.

Attitude and faith go hand-in-hand. Without the attitude that we as a people were good enough to go to any school, live in any neighborhood, or be whatever God would have us be, faith would not have had a leg to stand on. Without faith, the dreams of our ancestors would not have been realized.

Stuff happens and it's not all good, but it's not all bad all the time. It is our attitude that decides how we survive it. There are mothers who were told that because of fibroids and miscarriages they would never have children, but their attitudes said different. There are women who have been raped and abused and survived to give their testimony to inspire others to not let the crimes committed against them define who God created them to be. There are people who grew up with learning disabilities and were told they were stupid who are now great writers and scholars because their attitude said they could learn.

It is your attitude that brings you through. It determines whether you view a setback as your destiny or as a challenge. It determines whether you will choose to love once more or close your heart to the possibility, too afraid to get hurt again. Your attitude is that intangible element that resides in you, guiding you through life's maze. It is your compass, providing direction to your inner greatness.

Personal Challenge: There is a saying your attitude matches your altitude. When you first meet people, you project a particular attitude that either says speak to me or stay away. How does your non-verbal interaction affect your present relationships? Look at how your response and ways of being inhibit your forward motion. Are you one of those people who declare that people have to just get to know you? Do you rarely smile but somehow expect people to know you are approachable and wonder why you don't have more friends? Just for a day, try smiling and saying "hi" to people you walk by or come in direct contact with, and see how it alters your attitude. I remember trying this when I was having a bad day, and it actually helped. Beyond the smile, also try for one day not saying anything negative about anyone or anything, including you. Change your attitude, and change your life.

Sight	Smell	Taste	Sound	Touch

Writing Prompt: At the end of the day, expand on the following prompt: When I smile….

Be More of You

It was a little eerie, the other day, when I heard my spirit clearly say, "be more of you." What exactly did that mean? I then heard, "step out." In retrospect, I am not sure which came first. I just know I could not ignore either message. The words appeared like an unfinished puzzle. The key to the puzzle was the word "more." More means I choose to walk in love and not in fear of the steps I must take toward my greatness.

To be more means to not get comfortable in being less than who I am meant to be. To be more means to take a risk on walking an unknown road with shoes made of faith. While on financial leave from college, I remember my first job as a National and Foreign News Clerk at the *Atlanta Journal-Constitution*. My ambition at the time was to become a reporter, so the job was great. One day, I was on the elevator with a woman named Pam who I considered my mentor. She turned to me with a look of disappointment and said "you are becoming complacent." Her words rocked me because I knew she was right. She was right because my priorities had shifted from finishing school to just getting paid. I knew I had to make a move or else I would find myself like some of my peers who were unhappy and felt trapped by obligations that counted on their decent pay, good benefits, and occasional perks. I did not want to wake up 10 years later without a degree or the book I planned to write. To be uncomfortable in the unknown was just the push I needed. When I am uncomfortable, I become creative and exploit all of my abilities. I reach for more of me.

To be more means living without limits. I got up one morning and read a book entitled *The Prayer of Jabez*. Part of the prayer says: "Oh that you would bless me indeed and enlarge my territory." If you do not ask, you cannot receive. There is so much more out there for you if you believe in the possibility. There is more love and more joy if you ask for it. My bank account does not measure my possibilities, only my attitude. The universe is your playground, so hop on every swing, slide, jungle gym, or roll around in the grass if you want. Your life is only limited by the artificial boundaries your mind creates. When you look out at the ocean, you do not see an end. It has no (visible) boundaries, and even when artificial obstacles are constructed to restrict the water's movement, it is able to gather enough of its own strength to topple the best man-made design. You have to be like the water, and break the boundaries that constrict your movement.

To be more of me means to listen closely when spirit speaks. To be more means to reach for the best of me. To be more of me means I am not afraid to ask for what I want or the territory I need to see grow. To be more of me means I step out and do what God moves me to do. When you are being more, you cannot except less than what God has for you.

Personal Challenge: Today do that one thing you have hesitated to do because you think you don't have enough in your educational or financial storehouse.

Sight	Smell	Taste	Sound	Touch

Writing Prompt: I am more….and then dress it up with clothes.

The Best Fairytale

I'm not sure what the impetus was for me to throw away all of my harlequin romance books and declare: "ain't no prince riding on a white horse in the ghetto down 52nd St., not even on a ten-speed bike to save me." Perhaps I need to consult my old diaries to find out what shook me out of my Cinderella fantasies. I just remember being mad and empowered at the same time. It was for this reason that I never introduced my daughter to Cinderella, Snow White, or any of those "fair maidens" from my childhood that not only did not look like me, but also damaged my psyche with the belief in a dream that someone will rescue and take care of me. The damage was already done; because even though I threw away the books, I did not totally dismiss the possibility of the fairytale coming true.

Anyone who knows me knows I LOVE love! I have never given up on love; it just needs to be focused in some concrete reality that does not require me to give up myself. Whenever I shifted from this truth and slipped into a fairytale, I found myself in relationships where I was scuffling back to reclaim me or short changing the dreams I had for myself. The fairy dust made my eye sight blurry. I couldn't see what I gave up letting someone else take care of my needs and not my wants. I lost the focus on me.

My favorite book after I discarded my harlequin books was James Baldwin's *If Beale St. Could Talk*. I could wrap my mind and heart around these characters who found love in the midst of urban decay. Their love was a ride-or-die kind of love made from struggle and one which let each person grow and discover the self. Once I made it to Spelman, I was turned on to Paule Marshall, Rosa Guy, and

Toni Cade Bambara before falling head over heels for Zora Neale Hurston's *Their Eyes Were Watching God*. I wanted Teacake—a man so sweet he wasn't afraid to let me discover and to honor myself. I wanted a man who did not want me to show up as someone else or try to change me into his ideal once he believed he owned me. I needed to be whole like Janie, in Hurston's novel, grew to be—a self-actualized woman, which is why I love me some *Sula*. I teach this novel by Toni Morrison every year for my young women to learn the importance of loving your sisters and loving yourself and for my young men to learn why it is important for women to learn this lesson in order for men to be totally and fully loved. I want to encourage them to be like Ajax's character; a free man who loved a woman he believed to be brilliant and who did not confuse love with possession.

I gave my daughter both Hurston and Morrison's books. I informed her possession is antithetical to love and that a person must be free enough to love themselves to have some love to share. Love is not a commodity to be bartered or to be bought. Once love is up for sale, then so is the self which means the purchaser reserves the right to dismantle or decide to return it if it does not act right. I let her know, I don't come with a return label or any other kind of label or warranty. I am too valuable to be bought which is why I had to disallow any thoughts of knights in shining armor.

So when my daughter decided to marry, I informed her and her husband that in order for their marriage to work, a space must be created and respected for her to become a self-actualized woman. I let her husband know his happiness rested on her knowing she is more than a mother and more than a wife. It means, before either of those roles emerged, the Creator put her here with a plan and a purpose which

53

exceeds those roles. It means it is her duty to find that thing that brings her personal joy beyond a man or a baby. It is a mandate for her to live on purpose in order to earn her space on this planet. She has something unique to bring that has never been seen before, and I am sitting on the edge of my seat waiting for her to discover it and to share it.

Because I made sure from the time she was born that she had all the "paints and clay" she needed to paint and mold her world. This is not to say love is not necessary or needed; it is to say, loving up on her is mandatory and everything and anyone else that comes after is what makes a really good fairytale.

Chapter 4

MY BEAUTY

A Beautiful Change

(A post note on the Obamas ascension to the White house)

Let's be real, President Obama brings change not only because he is the first Black President but also because unlike a majority of high profile Black men, he has a mocha colored, statuesque, curvaceous, Black woman on his arm. Black is back, not in a corner, hidden in a closet, or slipping down a back stairway. Michelle Obama is front and center as the first Black First Lady of the United States.

Her beauty does not hail from a Halle Berry clone, nor is she a Beyoncé double. Her beauty represents the masses of beautiful Black women who have been overlooked or pushed aside. Don't get it wrong! There is plenty of love for the sisters of a lighter hue, but mass media already works overtime keeping them on a pedestal. What there has never been is enough visibility and praise for the darker sisters, who are just as or more beautiful as their sisters of a lighter hue. There has not been enough brown and dark-skinned little girls who are told early in life that they are beautiful and worthy so that they grow to believe it. As painful as this truth is, there are little Black girls and Black women who never garner the same attention as their lighter-skinned counterparts.

Outside of Denzel Washington and Samuel Jackson, there are not too many high profile Black men that come to my mind who show love for the darker sisters. Most high-profile, successful Black men believe the ultimate prize to go along with their accomplishments is a light or white symbol of beauty. Now we even see the media joining in by pairing Black men on serial dramas, like *The Practice*, with white

57

women instead of their Black female co-stars. The detriment of these images is the message it sends to Black youth. I remember standing in line at CVS watching two little boys giggle about how ugly they thought a Black female celebrity was in a magazine. I looked at the woman, her dark complexion, compelling eyes, laid hairdo and could not figure out how what they saw was unattractive, so I asked them why they thought she looked funny. The boys pointed to her broad, painted lips, her African features and said, "Look at them." If only the little boys knew how they had been conditioned to hate what others have grown to love. The "others" love it so much they get collagen shots in their lips so they too will have an attractive pout. I then asked them to show me a woman they thought was beautiful, and their choice was someone light-skinned with Caucasian features.

It is not their fault. Their choices have been picked by the same mass media outlets that convince little white girls to become anorexic in order to be seen as beautiful. Their choices are shaped by the images they see on television and in print that showcase bony, light-skinned, video vixens to excite the imaginations and hormones of little boys.

Since the Obamas have been in office, I now hear several of my Black male students proudly saying, "I'm looking for my Michelle," while the Black girls say they are looking for their "Obama." For the first time, what they seek is a full package that is not dependent on skin complexion but one built on substance. The Obama's image offers a change of the image of a Black man as a provider, father, and companion to his wife. Michelle changes the image of the dark-skinned sapphire, caricature to show a Black woman who supports her husband and nurtures her children while holding down the job of First Lady. Michelle represents another layer of the change President Obama brings; a change in seeing that the beauty of Black womanhood goes much deeper than the complexion of her skin, but the respect that first extends from the self then to her man and world community.

Personal Challenge: Make a list of at least 10 women in your family or community you see as beautiful. List the attributes that make them beautiful. Make sure you are on the list too. Beauty is not always a tangible thing or idea. Think about what makes your community beautiful and how you add to its beauty. Think about beauty as a circle of being.

Sight	Smell	Taste	Sound	Touch

Writing Prompt: My circle of beauty is…..

Belly Fat

Although it has been 23 years since I gave birth to a
9lb, 10oz lovely baby girl, I still blame her for my belly fat. I
look at pictures of me in my 20s showing off my sexy flat
belly in bikinis and midriff tops. It wasn't until my late 20s
that I started to notice a slight bulge begin to emerge. I
blamed it on a lack of exercise and taking for granted that for
most of my life, I could eat as much as I wanted without
gaining a pound. Losing it was never a problem. Plus, my
sassy older aunt Christine told me: "men like a little belly," so
I thought I was good.

The truth is the older I became, the more the fat
began to creep up on me and circle itself around me while I
slept. I even wrote a poem called "Beyoncé and the Body
Snatchers" and performed it on YouTube:
https://youtu.be/iO3Rn-6q6jY telling Beyoncé to give me
my body back. I was convinced of a conspiracy, an optical
illusion that tricked me decade-after-decade until I woke up at
50 horrified with the loose flab hoovering above and
protecting my most private parts. Therefore, I decided as
part of my 50 things to do at 50, I would lose the belly fat and
have a tasteful nude photo taken of me.

After having my daughter at 30, I began to think, it
was now or never to get back to my pre-pregnancy body. I
hired a personal trainer who threw away my chicken wings
and worked me until my abs showcased more muscle then
flab. I then fired the trainer and tried to go it alone. It has
been a struggle ever since with me hiring and firing new
trainers over and over again once I began to lose the weight.
Every time I see Angela Basset and/or Michelle Obama, I
renew my energy to lose the extra weight. That doesn't last

long. Eventually, I return to joking about it being "baby fat." Yet, the feel of my belly sitting on my thighs, or the surprise I feel when I see my naked body makes me feel like I've just given up on me—especially when I compare myself to other women my age. In fact, on social media, there are pictures of iconic stars over 50 who showcase their beautiful and timeless frames. At first, I was in awe, and then it occurred to me that the one thing all these women have in common are their bank accounts which enable them to employ personal chefs and trainers. Hell, if looking good was an essential part of my job, I wouldn't be asking Beyoncé' to give me my body back!

Recently, I developed some old Kodak film I found buried away in a plastic bag on the top shelf of my closet. Once the pictures were developed, I was amazed to find pictures of me at 20, 30, and 40 years old. I looked good!!!! There was actually a picture of me in my 30s posing on the sands of St. Maarten in a bikini! What and who was I comparing myself to in my late 20s when I thought I needed to lose 10 pounds, 20 pounds in my 30s, or 30 pounds in my 40s? In not one of these pictures did I look overweight. The one thing linking all these pictures together was me wearing my body well and feeling good enough to take the pictures. The reflection smiling back at me was not thinking about losing weight or thinking she needed to lose weight to look like Angela Basset or Beyoncé. I could say that some of my weight anxiety might be blamed on me being single. But looking at those pictures, I clearly saw how my being single had nothing to do with my size but everything to do with how I felt about my body weight as I aged. I shook my head in disbelief at all the time I wasted not appreciating my body in each decade.

I was so busy comparing myself to others who looked how I thought I should look that I missed out on me. I had buried my reflection and tucked it away at the top of my closet looking in other folks' mirrors in search of me. A friend once said: "whenever you strike comparisons between yourself and others, you will always come up short." I had neglected my own vision for so long I couldn't see me.

I am still single, and I never took that picture when I turned 50. After breaking my toe and finding out from the doctor that I was 214 pounds, I lost 20 pounds not to get a man but to get back to a healthy me. I no longer care if I am able to compete with Beyoncé-like body shapes who are my age. I'm ready to strike a pose at any age.

Personal Challenge: Think about who is in your mirror. Are you looking at you, or are you looking at what you think others might see? I challenge you to look at yourself as perfect in your present state. God did not make a mistake making you. Own that idea, and look at you with new eyes seeing you the way God sees you as a perfect creation.

Sight	Smell	Taste	Sound	Touch

Writing Prompt: In my mirror I see...

Figure Out the Goal

When I first decided to hire a personal trainer, my friend told me: "if you let someone else be your mode of motivation, you're relying on false methods [...] it's all in your head whether you keep running or pushing your body when it's telling you it wants to quit." He went on to tell me that the little black dress I'm dying to fit back into should be the fringe benefit—not the goal. The goal should be getting my body in shape. How I manage to reach the goal will determine the long-term benefit.

I hired Norris, my trainer, because I knew I needed extra motivation to get out of bed and exercise. Ironically, when I began to cry out in pain, my trainer re-phrased my friend's words. Norris told me that it is all about wrapping my mind around the goal. The first five laps around the track are simply preparation to complete the last two, which are the ones that really count, because then I've reached my goal. In order to reach my goals, I needed strategy and preparation. Without these, I might lose the weight but also lose sight of the goal which is to become physically fit.

Strategy and preparation assist in achieving the goal. The trick is figuring out the goal. Sure I want to fit back into the little black dress, and all the other clothes, wrapped in plastic, waiting to return to the front of the closet. But what would be different from the last time I lost weight? I'm clear I will not recover the body I had when I was 20, but the goal is my health. I've joined a gym, but it has been hard for me to continue working past the pain. I've cleansed and had colon hydrotherapy, which made me feel better and become aware of the foods that pollute my body, but I didn't lose the weight. I even hired Norris before, but wasn't able to keep my cut abs from becoming excess flab. What was my goal then? Was the goal to lose the weight to appease my vanity or to become healthy? Did I go through the cleansing to rid my body of built up waste, or was I hoping to drop 5 or 10 pounds? There is a difference in your performance when you figure out your goal.

Recently, one of my professors instructed me to re-write the introductory paragraph of my paper three times. Each time I came back to her, I was sure it was perfect. The disappointment I felt going back-and-forth is hard to relate. Mentally, I was fatigued and discouraged. The bottom line was I had to get it right, and I knew if I got what she was trying to show me, I could then teach someone else. At first I was trying to get the A, but after a few sessions I knew her goal was greater—to make me qualified to teach others. Once I wrapped my mind around the goal of being trained as future faculty, the fatigue disappeared, and I was no longer discouraged.

One of my best friends, Denise (Diva D), has talked about being a shoe designer since we were in high school, and she even went to London to learn the craft. A struggling entrepreneur, she has had to work other jobs to survive. Now, she has switched gears and decided not to take jobs that make others wealthy and deviate her from her goal. Becoming clear about her goal, she is buckling down to make shoes.

At the beginning of the New Year, I overheard a woman tell someone that she wasn't telling anyone about her goals because she didn't want to disappoint God if she didn't follow through. She may disappoint herself, but not God. God has a different goal in mind for her. God's goal is for her to reach the best in herself.

Goals are about realizing your personal best, whether that means achieving a healthy living plan, starting a new business, getting a new job, going back to school, getting all As, planning a vacation with a special person, or redefining relationships that work best for you. Your goal may be to find peace, so you can preserve a piece of mind. Whatever your goal is let it be about claiming the best in you.

God wants you to remember the 3 Ps as strategies to reaching your goals: prayer, perseverance, and persistence. Remember these strategies when the demands on your spirit, body, and mind buckle under pressure. Remember them when naysayers insert their points of view or that Snickers Bar starts calling you from across the room. When you figure out the goal, it makes lining up the strategies simple and achieving them easier. Through perseverance, I continue to exercise and commit to a new eating plan, with the goal of maintaining a healthy life style, knowing the little black dress is only the fringe benefit.

The goal must be something that grounds you in the task, feeds your spirit, and sparks your energy. Figure out the goal that inspires you to run that last lap when your side is cramping from the challenge. Saying you're going to do something because it's a new year or because somebody else told you to is quite different from *you* figuring out what's best for you. When you figure out the goal, you figure out how to reach the best in you—for you—in order for you to get it done.

Personal Challenge: Write a list of 5–10 goals you want to accomplish. After you compose your list, beside each goal write the purpose. For instance, do you want to lose weight to fit in an outfit or to become healthy? Is your goal to go to college to get a better paying job or to prove to yourself you can do it? Your true purpose in achieving the goal is what will give you the energy to complete it. Don't attach a wrong or right to your purpose, just think about if the purpose is strong enough for you to give the right amount of energy. One way to know if this is the purpose it when it inspires your ambition to reach your goal.

Sight	Smell	Taste	Sound	Touch

Writing Prompt: I am a source of inspiration who......

Love's Season

If I thought I'd only get love one day out of the year, I don't think I would want it. If I thought love only showed itself because of a funny looking kid named Cupid, I don't think I would consider it at all. Valentine's Day is good as a commercial venture but is a sad commodity. To think there needs to be a day put aside to remind you to show others you love them when sometimes you ain't lovin' you boggles my mind.

Whenever I think about Valentine's Day, I can't help but to think of the poem, "I hate valentine's day" written by my sister-friend Toni Blackman. When she writes, "we're all suckers anyway/ celebrating holidays and days that/ don't move us forward" I decided I didn't want to be considered a "sucker" again. Of course, I like the commercial trappings that come with the celebration; I just don't like being trapped or trapping others in the belief that love arrives in neat, red bows. Love's arrow does not always hit its intended target or even know which way to aim. Most of the time, who you love is as much a surprise to you as it is to them; and according to Toni, "who wants to be shot with a damn bow /and arrow." I understand why Toni hates the principle of Valentine's Day because love is not as neat and tidy as a bow; sometimes it unravels right before your eyes if not knotted from within.

Love cannot be packaged or bought. The love you give is the love that wakes up inside you. It does not wait on a special day to announce its presence because you are the present that keeps on giving. Not knowing this causes you to be depressed because you are looking for love to sit beside you rather than inside you.

Love is a year round resident, not a temporary occupant. It cannot reside in a space cluttered with guilt. Guilt is the residue of the past that you cannot change. It is something that you allow to make your heart heavy and cut off your air. Love cannot freely move in a heart with arteries clogged by resentment and fear. It needs a clear passage. It needs a space to filter out and inhale positive, instead of negative, air.

You are your first Valentine. You absolutely cannot give what you do not have. Some of the most loving people I know are not people with a significant other on their arm but people who are significant to themselves. If Valentine's Day serves any purpose, let it be to remind you to love you out of season and for no other reason than because....

Personal Challenge: No matter how you feel today, write at least 20 ways you are love. Only speak love into every situation today. Only see yourself and others as sources of love's light and the many ways it shows itself. At the end of your day, expand on the writing prompt below.

Sight	Smell	Taste	Sound	Touch

Writing Prompt: I love me in and out of season...

Chapter 5

MY WORTH

Validation

There are a lot of different barriers which keep us from moving forward in this world. Looking for validation for our efforts outside of ourselves is a sure way to impede progress and to ensure low self-esteem.

What is it that makes what we think about ourselves as not enough? Why is it that we need someone to be a cosigner on how bright, pretty, or good we are? True, there are some who don't give a damn about what others think of them and keep on pushing forward, becoming shinning stars. Yet, after doing the work, persevering rather than running, taking bold steps, they too can trip up and fall victim to self-doubt. They too may stop and ask: "am I on the right path?" "Am I worthy of the praise I receive?" "Do I deserve the money I'm making for such easy work?" "Do people really like me?"

There is nothing wrong with a little self-inventory. The problem arises when how we feel about ourselves can only be countered by outside forces whose critique is far more valuable than our own. Thus, we have given over our power to someone else. There is a woman who made the comment that she was not validated as a woman because she had not been married nor had children. So then, what was she? God created her as a woman; any doctor who would examine her would say she was a woman, but she couldn't embrace her womanhood because of outside standards she had chosen to believe. The same goes for the person who draws wonderful portraits and doesn't think they are an artist because no one told them they were, or because they haven't sold a painting. God has given him or her talent, but because someone else doesn't say "its art," they roll up the canvases and throw away the paints.

No one should be given the authority to direct or to design our destiny. We should never hand someone that power by predicating our abilities on the stamp of approval *they* give. If you were called to fulfill a certain task on Earth, then fulfill it! If you were meant to dance, dance! If you were given a voice that sings babies to sleep, sing! If your gift is to paint, draw, teach, count money, or show other people their dreams, then do that!

You can't count on a mentor to take you under their wing. You can't count on your friends to understand your dreams or determination. You can't count on that particular person whose opinion you have deemed important to "get it," they just might not. And if they don't, that needs to be okay too. Because whatever you've done, whether it's created a new management system or invention, it was God inspired. It was meant for you to do, and YOU have to believe you did the best job within your abilities; anything else is out of your control.

I remember some years ago asking God to give me a sign to let me know if writing was what I was supposed to be doing. Within the same month, I was simultaneously gifted with a city-wide young writer's Bronze Jubilee Award and a grant from the Georgia National Arts Council to publish my first book of poetry *Slightly Off Center*. However, this wasn't enough because I found myself, a few years later, during a rough patch of life, asking the same question again: "Is writing my purpose?" It was then that I had to stop and to remember. I asked myself how many times I was going to ask myself the same question. How many times did I need to receive the same answer to believe it? I now understand that my faith in self was so corrupt, I couldn't even accept validation from God; the One who called me to the task.

Now in times of doubt, I simply remember the words that came to me on the edge of sleep, "whatever is God inspired is God sent." Just as my words are sent by God so am I. We are one. One cannot be separated from the other. God was inspired to create all of us and to send us forth into the world. We were birthed with different gifts and abilities, all God inspired and God sent. Outside validation is nice, but not necessary to do the work we were sent here to do. Validation is a long word for value. If we value our gifts and abilities, then the hard part is done because we were validated first by God, and in the Most High's eye, we are all valuable and worthy of praise.

Personal Challenge: When you question or seek validation, you are questioning your worth. Look to see what has occurred in your past that you are letting live in your present to question your worth. Validation is a worth question; how do you seek validation? How does gaining or not gaining validation stop you from achieving your goals? Let's change the script.

Sight	Smell	Taste	Sound	Touch

Writing Prompt: My Worth is…..

Remember My Name

When you
remember my
walk upon this
earth
Look not into
my steps with
pity.
When you
taste the tears
of my journey
Notice how
they fill my
foot prints
Not my spirit
For that
remains with
me.
My story must
be told
Must remain in
conscious
memory
So my
daughters
won't cry my
tears
Or follow my
tortured legacy.
Lovin'
is a tricky thing
If it doesn't
come
from a healthy
place,

If Lovin'
Doesn't FIRST
practice
on self
it will act like a
stray bullet
not caring
what it hits
You may say:
Maybe I
should've
loved him a
little less,
Maybe I
should've
loved me a
little more,
Maybe I
should've not
believed he'd
never hit me
again.
All those
maybes will
not bring me
back – not
right his
wrong.
My life was not
his to take.
As your eyes
glance my
name

Understand
once I
breathed
Walked
Loved
just like you.
I wish for all
who glance my
name
To know love
turned fear –
kept me there
Loved twisted
to fear,
Kept me in a
chokehold
Cut off my air
Blurred my
vision
I couldn't see
how to break
free.
I shoulda told
my family
I shoulda told
my friends
I shoulda got
that CPO
Before the
police let him
go
But all those
shoulda's can't
bring me back

when I lied so
well
To cover the
shame
To hide the
signs.
If my death
had to show
what love isn't
If my death
had to show
that love
shouldn't hurt
If my death
had to make
sure

another
woman told a
friend
instead of
holding it in
If my death
reminds you
how beautiful
how worthy
you really are
If my death
reminds you
to honor all
you are
daily

Then
remember my
name
Shout it
from the
center of your
soul
Wake me
in my grave
Let ME know
My LIVING
was not in
vain.

A Sorry Lie

It was a nice sunny day, and I was playing outside in front of my house, as a child, when a tall, nice looking woman dressed in a black halter top with tight black pants ran past me crying. Following her was a man with a thick, black, leather belt wrapped around his fist, like the kind I hid in the basement after my last spanking from my father. When I saw him swing the belt and hit her legs, I jumped. No one on the street did anything. Years later, when I was a teenager, I was walking across the 49th St. bridge in Philly when I saw a big woman in a nurses uniform curled in a ball on the ground being punched and kicked by a squirrel of a man in the light of day. I wondered why she didn't get up and sit on him?

Once I became grown, I realized the size or beauty of a woman doesn't matter when she is beat from the inside. Before a fist lands, words hit to deaden the spirit to make the woman believe she is worthless and deserves the punishment she receives. It was not until I was hired as the first employee for The D.C. Coalition against Domestic Violence to spread the word about the warning signs and cycle of domestic violence that I understood these events are not as rare as what I witnessed in my childhood.

I understood that abuse is a secret victims cannot keep. I understood why women get beat in the light of day without anyone coming to their rescue. I understood why every day a woman dies at the hands of a man who said he loved her. It was through that work, that I learned how women are groomed to accept the violence of charismatic men who claim they love them. They are vulnerable when they are not aware of the warning signs that include jealousy, short tempers, the need to control what a woman wears, her activities, and the need to isolate the woman from family and friends. As a result, I ask my partners in advance how they handle their anger.

When I spoke to groups, they often asked me: why does she stay? I asked: why does he beat her? I also explained that women are at a higher risk when they leave and need support to plan a safe departure. There are many other factors such as children and the need to believe the man she loves means it when he says he is sorry and will not hit her again. When I wrote the "Remember My Name" poem in 1995, it was after hearing the stories of women in prison who killed to protect themselves. It was after hearing stories of women repeating a cycle begun by their mothers believing a man was not a man unless he could control her with a punch. It was after hearing stories of daughters and sons who lost their mothers to their father's anger or her lover's rage. It was after witnessing the many lost lives sewn in a quilt of sadness for women who believed their man's sorry lie.

Personal Challenge: In many of these cases, the first lie is the lie you tell yourself. It is the lie that you do not deserve more and a belief that what he says about you and to you is the truth. When you first met, he was attracted to the glow in your eyes and the power in your walk. It is that power that the heel of his boot seeks to stomp out, so he can feel more powerful. I challenge you to remember who you were before him and to remember the person you always knew you could be.

Sight	Smell	Taste	Sound	Touch

Writing Prompt: I remember me…..

Self-Compassion

Recently, I faced an awesome challenge that had the power to shake what I believed about myself and my purpose. When I shared what I saw as a failure with a few close friends, they all thought I was being hard on myself. One friend just said: "on with the next adventure!" The compassion my friends and family showed me was much more than what I showed myself.

It was during a yoga class that I first honed in on the meaning of compassion. I thought compassion was something you give to other people. When the instructor cautioned us to be compassionate with our bodies and their ability to function in the movements, my hand immediately moved to my ankle. I broke my ankle earlier that year and thought the more I pushed, the quicker my ankle would get back to normal.

I needed to have compassion with what my body and mind were telling me it needed. For instance, if my body is tired then I need to go to sleep and not guilt myself into trying to do more in that day then my body is able. The other day, my mother complained that she didn't want to do anything but lay in the bed. I said "why not? You worked all your life, you're retired and don't have to worry about how the bills will get paid—so lay there." Guilt is overrated and overused by folks who are afraid to own what they feel.

Having compassion for myself means I respect my choices even if my choice means choosing me despite of how it may disappoint someone else. I have learned having compassion for my healing, my growth, and my journey is the best way to honor the God in me.

Personal Challenge: Today, be patient with your process, and honor how you feel. You cannot expect anyone to give you the compassion you do not give yourself. When you are not compassionate with yourself, you are not valuing yourself. Look into your Come from Place. Where were you criticized or told you were not enough? Sometimes being compassionate is confused with being lazy or not challenging yourself. Let's flip the script. When you are compassionate with yourself, you give yourself time to breathe, refresh goals, dreams, and energy.

Sight	Smell	Taste	Sound	Touch

Writing Prompt: I honor the God in me…..

Sister Love

This is not about the backlash I heard R&B singer Rhianna receive after detailing the abuse she suffered at the hands of a man she thought loved her. This is not about my female students who I spoke to about teaching another sister about being a better sister rather than alienating her from the group. My concern is about how sisters overall must love themselves better in order to be better sisters to one another.

In a poem I wrote to my mother I said, "Everything I learned about being a sister I learned from you." Part of what she taught me was that it is alright to compliment a sister when she looks good. It is also alright to keep your sisters close even while "He" is around because, after "He" is gone, more than likely your sisters will be there. They will be the ones to remind you that you are still beautiful and worthy when "He" disappears. When "He" removes his shoulder as a place for your head to rest your troubles on, nine times out of ten, your sisters will be there to remind you a better day is coming.

I really don't have much patience for sisters who do not know the value of sisterhood. I remember my initiation into the Spelman sisterhood and how awesome we were in our white as one collective body. I took the ceremony seriously and although I did not graduate from there, my sense of sisterhood did. I have and know sisters who know the bond of sisterhood that reaches beyond those iron gates. Trust, I have been careless in some of my relationships with my sister-friends. I remember being so in love with a guy that I neglected my weekly sister chats. I put our relationship on the back burner until I needed her to be my co-pilot to jet down the highway to retrieve my belongings. Through our laughter, she admonished me with love to never forget your sisters because sisters have your back after the man is gone. It is for this reason I have allowed sisters into my circle who have not read the sisterhood memo. When they say they are without sister-friends, I ignore the red flag and take up the charge to show them real sisters do exist. It is my intent to share the value of the love I learned. Sadly, I have also learned everyone isn't able to be a sister to another sister.

When I became less reckless with the care I had for myself, I was less reckless with the care I had for my sisters. See, you can't take care of one without the other. There is no way I can give excuses for a man beating a woman if I would not first excuse the behavior for myself. If I know love should not hurt, if I know that regardless of what I say, no man has the right to hit, push, shove, kick, or spit on me, then there is NO way I will condone this behavior toward a sister! My response to my sisters' well- being is a response to what I believe I deserve for myself.

The inability to love and to take care of my sister is ultimately a reflection of the love I have for myself. I want no less for my sister than I want for myself. The MORE I want for her is the MORE I want for me: more love, happiness, understanding, gratitude, purpose, patience; more of the MORE the Most High has designed for me.

Personal Challenge: Too often women do not complement one another. Today give at least five women you come in contact with a compliment. Do not utter a negative idea or opinion about another sister, including you.

Sight	Smell	Taste	Sound	Touch

Writing Prompt: I am My Sister's Keeper...

Chapter 6

FORGIVE FOR YOU

You Can't Throw People Away

One of the wisest women I never met, except through our conversations on the telephone was my friend Vincent's mother, Mrs. Pouge. I would spend so much time hearing her stories that sometimes I forgot I had called to speak to her son. Eventually, I began to call her to just speak to her to gather some of her wisdom about a particular issue which is what I was doing when I asked her about putting family members on time out. Mrs. Pogue told me: "you can't throw people away." Although she has been dead several years, her words still haunt me, especially during the holidays when we notice members of the family who are missing because of our wishes or their own. Mrs. Pogue reminded me that we *can* pick our friends but not our family.

Still, this notion confounds me. I wonder about those family members who are in so much personal pain they become toxic to my spirit. I wonder about the ones that seem to never get it together and to always need someone to pick them up. I wonder about the ones we can't trust to leave in our home alone. And then, I considered the Prodigal Son. The son who left, squandered his riches, returned home, broke and in want. While his brother was resentful, the father was grateful for his return. The father's heart was such that he could embrace his son regardless of what he had done.

Some horrific atrocities happen in families today, which make it even harder for Mrs. Pogue's words to be accepted. Yet, to act as if we are not connected to people who share our blood line is to negate a part of ourselves, part of the tree we come from. Part of embracing ourselves must be about embracing all of us; even those family members we wish didn't belong to us. Everyone doesn't deserve to be in the front row in our arena, but shouldn't there be a door open that allows for entry? Too often we give much more leniency to friends who disappoint us than to our own family. Why do we expect our families to be perfect? They are made up of people who experience individual traumas, setbacks, and just plain "life stuff." I think our expectations are warped by T.V. Land: John Walton, The Brady Bunch, and Cosby Show fantasies. Get over it, nobody is perfect.

Some of us have drug addicts or alcoholics as cousins, uncles, aunts, mothers, or fathers. Because they do not live up to our expectations as law-abiding citizens, do we throw them away? Some of us are embroiled in family feuds that affect younger relatives who don't even understand the beef. Do we continue fighting at the risk of dissolving family ties forever? Some of us will not communicate with family members because of real or unreal disappointments and hurts. When do we look at our own part in the friction and decide that family is bigger than us and get over it? During Thanksgiving, I had a cousin who was not planning on attending the annual event because he didn't want his toxic feelings to infect the family. Upon his arrival, after the first joke, he realized being in isolation was what his mind had tricked him into believing he wanted, being around family is what he needed. He said: "I forgot I needed maintenance." Sometimes being able to accept the love from family means we have to accept ourselves. Most of the time the negative stuff family members are giving us has nothing to do with us; they just forgot they needed maintenance.

I get pissed off at family members who think everything is about them and always want to look at the negative sides of family without ever considering or looking for the good. And it always seems like the ones who know the entire Bible judge and cast members out without any hope of their being able to redeem themselves. Stuff happens, and we cannot expect family members to be any more perfect than we are. To heal myself, I had to go to family members and lay bare my grievances to forgive myself and them. Families are work, and we must be willing to do the work. Families are how we as African Americans have been able to survive in a country that has often tried to exterminate us. Families are our life lines. We cannot throw them away. Love them from a distance if the situation calls for it, but be open to the possibility of change within them and within ourselves. Compassion and forgiveness are what we ask from God, but how can we expect to receive what we cannot give? At the end of the day, all we have is family. When we fall from grace, God is there to lift us up and encircle us within a circle of love. Who are we not to do the same for our circle of family?

Personal Challenge: Sometimes it appears a family member needs a time out, but when the time out takes longer than a year, it might be time to revisit the possibility of how to bring that member back into the fold. Without having any expectations or condemnations, compose a letter of possibilities to your family member. Write it as if you will mail or give it to them. Use the prompt as your guide.

Sight	Smell	Taste	Sound	Touch

Writing Prompt: Everything in this letter must speak in the positive. You are not to use the letter to say things like: "I look forward to the possibility of you not pissing me off when I see you."

Instead it should read: "Dear Cousin/Sister, I am open to the possibility of healing and to the possibility that you will join me on this journey of healing so we don't miss the good in one another." Begin each sentence with the possibility you are putting out into the world. Remember your positive intention of healing as you write. Try not to bring up the fights and areas of contention because you both remember those moments differently and it will block the listening and the genuine receipt of your message.

92

Renegotiating Relationships

While waiting for his wife to return from a shopping adventure, I asked my mentor, Bob Hoffman, for the secret to his long and successful union with his wife. He looked at his watch, shook his head, and said it is "the ability to renegotiate the relationship at least every few years or like now, every six months." The renegotiation depends on the terms and growth of the relationship. I find that as I grow, as I evolve into the person I am destined to be, some of my closest relationships need to be renegotiated. The terms upon which they were created no longer fit who I am today.

All relationships are built on agreements. Parents make agreements with children, and as children grow, the terms of the agreements must be renegotiated to maintain healthy relationships. Husbands and wives agree to certain terms at the altar, which must be renegotiated as they grow as individuals to remain a couple. Siblings and friends, as they grow and mature, must revise the terms of their relationship. The terms of the agreement are made when people tell others how they like to be treated.

Recently, I read Gary Chapman's book, *The 5 Love Languages*. What the book made me realize most was how often people do not hear each other because they are not speaking a language the other person understands. Sometimes this is due to bad listening skills. Most of the time, it is because the person does not know or understand their own language well enough to articulate it to another person. If I do not understand my own love language, how can I expect someone else to understand? Moreover, how can I negotiate an agreement if there is a language barrier? I have to start with understanding my own language, so I can inform and negotiate the terms of an agreement in relationships with other people.

This particular lesson came home to me when I realized that instead of renegotiating relationship agreements, I was terminating them. I stopped myself and asked, "Why is this happening?" and "What is up with this pattern?" I later realized that I had not learned my love language nor articulated to others what is acceptable and what is not. Instead, because of my fear of confrontation, abandonment, and not being liked, I let others continue in their behavior. I tried to absorb the hurt and cover the wounds with: "They didn't mean it," "We'll get over that," or "It really isn't that big," until my shock absorbers wore out. I ran out of scabs, and my hurt refused to heal. Because of my fear of rejection and confrontation, I have walked around on egg shells in some of my relationships, scared folks would explode all over me if I should misstep. Yet, my tip-toe, tap-dance never halted the explosion. I still got egg on my face, wondering what I could have done differently, or how I could make them feel okay.

Reading and understanding *The 5 Love Languages* gave me another route toward loving myself and teaching people how to love me. I cannot blame people for treating me in a way that I had not defined as unacceptable. Not all contracts are renewable or should be renegotiated. When relationships are physically, mentally, or spiritually abusive, those relationships need to be cancelled without renegotiation. My job is to make sure I am in agreement with my terms and that they are clearly stated. I don't care if it's my mother, father, brother, sister, grandparent, best friend, or lover; people need to know how to treat me. How they respond to my terms and how I respond to theirs determines the outcome of the agreement.

I honor my spirit by refusing to let others take my kindness for weakness or to use me as a dumping ground for their own self-inflicted madness. I do not agree to allow others to project their insecurities and misplaced blame onto me because it is easier than self-investigation. Relationships take work. Before I negotiate or renegotiate a relationship with anyone else, I must first figure out my own terms of agreement. I must know what terms are non-negotiable. Once this is done, it is easier to sign on the dotted line.

Personal Challenge: Get a copy of Gary Chapman's *The 5 Love Languages*. For instance, I know one of my languages is acts of service. Now, sometimes this can trip me up because I'm thinking these acts mean love but for that person, it's just what they do. Assess your language, and begin to look at your relationships. Is there a pattern that needs to be interrupted? Make a list of your negotiable and non-negotiable acceptable behaviors. For example, using profanity or calling me out of my name during an argument is one of my non-negotiables. Consider that you are entering into a contract with yourself where you are able to detail the services you will provide from spirit and what your spirit will not allow you to provide. Use the prompt below to construct your personal contract.

Sight	Smell	Taste	Sound	Touch

Writing Prompt: Relationship Agreement

THIS AGREEMENT is entered into as of _____, 20__, by and between MYSELF, a complete and self-defined person whose principal office is located at (your residence)_____, and ___ME_____ in the State of _____ whose principal office is located _in spirit_____ (collectively, the "Parties").

SERVICES

I shall provide the following services for the Client ME to (general description): (enumerate the specific services) (collectively the "Services"). Exhibit A includes a summary of services:

Exhibit B includes a summary of services not provided by this contract.

COMPENSATION AND MANNER OF PAYMENT

The fee for the Services shall be (ex: Respect)_____ paid in (#) installments of_____.

I shall provide Me with_____ (#) invoices for (percentage) of the fee according to the following schedule: (this can be a schedule of the ways you will honor yourself or check in on your wellness). The Client (ME) shall pay each invoice no later than 10–15 days after the date of the invoice.

I shall provide Me with_____ (#) invoices for (percentage) of the fee according to the following schedule: (this can be a schedule of the ways you will honor yourself or check in on your wellness). The Client (ME) shall pay each invoice no later than 10–15 days after the date of the invoice.

TERMS AND TERMINATION

The initial term of this Agreement shall commence on _____ and continue until (ex: a life-time) _____.

This Agreement may be terminated by mutual agreement of the Parties hereto, or by either Party within five business days written notice.

Impressions

When I would see President Obama strut across the White House lawn or cast an approving smile to his wife and daughters, I was reminded of Black manhood and black love as a sustainable idea. The impression he gave us all is one of possibility. I do not always get that impression when I look at television images of Black men who appear hopeless, black women who appear unlovable, and both who appear in need of rescue by people who do not look like them. The impression these images leave on grown folks, still trying to find their way, and young folks who do not know the way are troubling and powerful. What is even more troubling is the impression we have control over and decide to leave on people without acknowledgement of the long term affect.

Every year, I am besieged by images presented by my freshmen classes that are in need of correction. I have students who come to my class glassy-eyed and smelling like a burning marijuana plant. I have young men showing me the Tweety Birds on their underwear and some young women who wear skirts that look more appropriate for a night club than a classroom. The impression they give is that they are not serious about their education. Some of these same students will need recommendation letters for internships and additional scholarships. They do not understand that how they report to the classroom is how they should report to a job: dressed appropriately, on time, and serious about the task at hand. They clearly do not understand the correlation between how they show up to class with how their instructors and other classmates perceive their ability and potential.

How we show up to a person decides whether we get a front row or back row seat in their arena. I remember joking with someone who did not find my joke funny. She had just met me and was not use to my sense of humor. I cannot remember the joke, but I do remember the impression it left her about me. When we crossed paths again, her face became tight as she acted like she did not know me. I will never have the opportunity to apologize or to show her a better side of me. Sometimes all we get is one opportunity. Seldom is there an opportunity for a do over.

What I learned from that encounter is to be mindful of the impression I leave with people. I try to make sure the impression I leave is the one I intend to give. Recently, I ran into two of male students I taught when they were in high school. During my individual conversations with them, they both told me they still had the journals I gave them for their graduation. It made me feel good that all these years later, I had left a good enough impression on them that they consider these gifts as valuable keepsakes. On the flip side, I have had to help a sister reconnect with someone because she knew that how she left the relationship was less than graceful. It was not hard for her to admit her wrong, but it was hard for her to believe that the person would speak to her again because of her actions. Once she explained that she was indeed projecting her issues onto the other person, all was forgiven, and they moved on.

Forgiveness is possible, but too often impressions are like indelible stains that are hard to remove. I wish I could grab back that moment when I unintentionally hurt someone's feelings, but I cannot. How I show up at particular time and space does not necessarily account for the sum total of me, but it is up to me to be cognizant of how I show up because when the curtain comes down, all people are left with is that last impression.

Personal Challenge: Look to see if there is a person or situation you have not forgiven. When you don't forgive, it is the same as a grudge that you have to remember in order to harbor the negative feeling toward someone or yourself. If there is more than one person or situation just pick one today to challenge yourself to forgive. You can choose to forgive you.

Sight	Smell	Taste	Sound	Touch

Writing Prompt: This is a letter you are writing either to yourself or the person you need to forgive. After you are finished, you can either keep it, burn it or give it to the person you need to forgive. Remember forgiveness is not for the other person but for you to move freely without the weight of the offense hindering your movements. Also, just because you forgive does not mean you forget.

Dear _____

I forgive ......

Stuck on Stupid

During a wedding toast, my mother always lends these words of advice: "communicate, communicate, and communicate." These words appear simple enough but are all too often forgotten. In the heat of misunderstandings words become stuck to the tongue making it ball up into a fist of silence. Each person waits for the other to blink so that they can claim the win. Stuck in a silent battle of rage each person builds their own narrative of understanding without consulting the other person. Each person is stuck in their version of what they think is right and true. The truth is no one can know what is right or true if the tongue isn't freed up to negotiate speech.

When you commit to silent battle, it's as if you are playing poker with your heart. You don't want the other person to know what's in your hand for fear that they may see your ace or that you don't have one. Everything is kept close to the chest. You only let one card show at a time. The only thing wrong with this strategy is that if you don't know when to fold, you may be left at the table by yourself. The only way to win in any relationship is to be all in it. You don't want to be vulnerable and sometimes you don't want to say the wrong thing, so you say nothing. Being stuck is fear based. You succumb to the fear of being misunderstood and the fear of being rejected once you let the other person know how you feel.

What is even crazier are the stories supported by the fear that begins to gather in the not so silent corners of your mind. Your imagination gathers wind and your mind takes flight to galaxies unknown to you and your unwilling passenger. Stories take on shapes and sizes that bolster what you believe to be right and true. You take one brick of the story without consideration of the other side and build a lopsided house. Once you have built a not so sturdy structure, you invite everyone over to inspect what your stories have created except the person you are angry with; the person whose story which is able to straighten the leaning structure. If you are lucky, a kind visitor will point out the cracks and the missing beams needed to support your house and suggest you consult your contractor or architect and then you realize you are missing a side. You are missing the side of the story that will clarify what you believe to be true. You are missing the dual rational for the behavior and you are missing the answers that will offer you the opportunity to grow from the fear of the unknown.

Friends, family members, husbands, wives, and significant others have been lost because hearts were unable to loosen stubborn tongues stuck in the fear of communicating truth. It is stupid to think someone else knows what is going on in your mind if you do not tell them. It is stupid to stay stuck in a place of misunderstanding because your ego refuses to let you be the person to blink or speak first. It is stupid to choose to remain stuck when it is so much easier to communicate, so you both can move forward however that may look. Releasing the tongue is releasing the fear, and releasing the fear is releasing the heart to do and to be more.

Personal Challenge: Release the need to be right and the fear of being wrong. When you try to have the last word or cannot release the need to convince another person to agree with your position, you become stuck. Somewhere along your path, the need to be right became equal to being smart. Knowing the right answer made you feel good and above others. Now, feel the freedom of not being attached to being wrong or right.

Sight	Smell	Taste	Sound	Touch

Writing Prompt: It is All Good....

Chapter 7

LOVE LETTER TO YOU

A Healing Letter to Self

While in the midst of a pity-party that I could not seem to shake, my father asked me: "if someone contacted you who was dealing with the same issue you're dealing with, what would you say to them? Pretend you're Dear Abby and answer them."

I pondered this idea and thought about how often I share my wisdom with others. It also occurred to me how often, when in the midst of my own nightmares, that same wisdom eludes me. So, I decided to take my father's advice and write a Dear Kimberly healing letter.

Dear Kimberly,

Recently I found out that someone I considered to be one of my best friends has been lying to me about who he is and about his feelings for me for years. I confided in him, loved him, even invited him into my immediate and extended family, and they also embraced him. I thought he had integrity and was worthy of my respect. Now I know he was just a smooth con artist.

My soul hurts. I don't know what to do with the pain. I feel like my picker is broken. I've known him for practically a decade, and now I question every word he spoke and his every action. It all appears to have been an orchestrated concert of deceit and manipulation to serve his need to have shelter, food, money, or a warm body when none other was available. I acted out of sincere friendship and love, and now I see that I have been like Dorothy in the Wizard of Oz, lost and believing in something that was not real. I am now trying to find my way home and out of this abyss of hurt, deceit, and rage. How do I heal and come home?

Sincerely,

Me

Dear Me:

First, be glad for clarity of vision. Sometimes, it's hard to see what's right in front of you, which is why you didn't heed the signs along the way. I suspect there were signs, but you chose not to see or believe them. You wanted to believe in the person you loved, and you weren't ready to feel truth's pain.

Loving someone is never a bad thing. Just because you love someone doesn't mean they will honor, appreciate, or even receive your love or treat you as their beloved. Love is not something we own; love is a power; a force that moves freely and, yes, love is shared among friends. You write that he was your "best friend." I think you were his best friend, but he was never yours.

In order to be a friend to others, you must first be a friend to yourself. It's likely he hasn't yet learned how. When you discovered the truth and chose to walk away, you were being a wonderful friend to you! You know what friendship feels like because you've practiced loving you. You've looked in the mirror and stared truth down while feeling truth's pain. Kimberly, your "picker" is not broken; you just chose to befriend someone whose heart and soul is broken. You tried to fix it with your love and friendship, but that is his work not yours.

I know your "soul hurts," and right now, it's hard to believe you will feel whole and well again. But you've been here before, so you know you will feel whole and well again. You know that what you're feeling right now will pass into a distant memory without a tingle of pain and that only the lesson will remain. The blessing for you is getting the lesson.

I know you want him to hurt as much as you and revenge seems like your BFF right now. But he will experience what he needs to experience as he walks his life's journey without any help from you. He, like you, like each of us is in need of healing, and we chart our own course as we travel. We all have the blessing of intuition to hear that whisper which is your God voice telling you to run the other way. When you don't listen, you get hurt. This is not the first time you have experienced this lesson. Perhaps the pain of remembering the lesson will teach you to pay attention and to not ignore God when she is speaking to you the next time.

So keep your heart muscles moving, and allow this experience to grow your heart stronger. In order to lose something, there must be something to win. You were the prize, not him. Your mind, soul, and spirit are all intact. He took nothing from you because he gave you nothing; he did not make you, God did. You are God's child, and she wants you to keep showing up in the world as the vehicle of love that she made you to be. With God as your friend, you will not need to click your heels three times. All you need to do is to let go of what is not of you. Remember, God and your ancestors dance because you are here, so you need to dance too—all the way home.

Personal Challenge: Name the experience or situation that challenges how you feel about yourself. Once you name the experience, address it as if you are a third-party offering advice to heal the soul of that experience to remind the soul of its beauty and worth. Sift through the difference between what has been told to you and what you believe to be true about yourself. The ability to change negative messages into positive messages is the first step toward switching out the inactive computer drive in your brain with a productive and new computer chip.

Sight	Smell	Taste	Sound	Touch

Writing Prompt: After you have completed your list, use at least one example from each column to begin your healing letter to self: Dear Me_____

Everybody Needs Dreams

"A Dream Deferred" Does it dry up
like a raisin in the sun?
Or fester like a sore-- And then run? [. . .]
Or does it explode?

-Langston Hughes

I was thoroughly moved by the movie Hustle and
Flow and its message: "Everybody gotta have a dream."
Without dreams you cannot create a vision. Dreams are what
you sleep on, walk through the days with, and save you when
you find yourself desperately holding onto a life line. They
are what nourish your existence and state of mind. Since I
was a child, incubated in dreams, they have been my mantra
for living.

What do you want? What do you dream? What have
you forgotten that God whispered in your ear at birth? Did
you ignore the gentle reminders along the way? Are your
dreams on lock down? Did you dismiss the dream 'cause
somebody told you it could not come true? A friend of mine
told me his reality check comes from looking at the homeless
on the street. He knows they were once children who played
and dreamed of becoming more. They are someone's child,
mother, sister, brother, or father, and you wonder, "what
happened" ? Why couldn't they bounce back? Sometimes
people have a really bad day that lasts longer than just a day.
Sometimes things get so crazy you can't remember words of
wisdom reminding you, "this too shall pass." Sometimes the
voices outside our heads are so loud that we forget our
dreams and decide to check out physically or mentally.

112

I grew up surrounded by dreamers. My father would weave his dreams around me, and I watched him make some of them come true. I also listened to people make fun of him, asking me what my father was going to be next. Their talk angered me because they thought his dreams were a joke, and I believed in those dreams and him. They angered me because they thought it was okay to make fun of a child's parent in a room full of people without him being there to defend himself. What they didn't know was my perception of them. I saw them as lacking in courage, not able to reach for dreams of their own. My father has always been larger than life to me because he has never let fear stop him from re-inventing himself and going after his dreams. My mother faced the same kind of ridicule on a different scale. Everyone was always proud of her academic achievements, but some questioned her lack of material items. The important thing was that she understood her priorities and achieved all and more than she dreamed for herself and for me.

Dreams have always fueled my passion and kept me on track. To me, dreams are like oxygen; fearing to dream is fearing to live, and what is life without oxygen? Dreams help you breathe while you work a job that does not foster who you are or is not reflective of you but merely helps you move toward to who you will become. What are the dreams that continue to circle your mind but get knocked down because you're scared they won't be realized?

Dreams remind you that you got a thing to do in this world. They nag you until you realize them or dismiss them. Everybody has a dream. Claim yours. Langston knew the power of claiming dreams. The ancestors built America on dreams, marched on a dream, sat in, got hosed down for a dream. Sometimes we gotta get desperate before we work on and realize our dreams—so what, as long as you make it happen. Do it, and fulfill the Most High's dream for you.

Personal Challenge: List the earliest dream you can remember that you had for yourself to present day. Do not edit your dreams according to what you know in your present reality, just list them. Once your list is complete, do not judge your dreams but insert them as you follow your writing prompt. Expand your chart of five tangible senses to also include colors, and then answer the writing prompt below.

Sight	Smell	Taste	Sound	Touch

<u>Writing Prompt</u>: I Dream of Me…or The Dream of Myself is…

Good Day

Ain't nothing like a good day. A day when you wake
up feeling God's smile arching your back forward to embrace
another chance to get it right. I have a collection of good
days. I remember the day my friend, Denise, and I started
out the day having brunch at a quaint café, then walking up
Spring Garden Street to the Parkway in Philadelphia, where
there was a party in the street. Jill Scott summoned us singing
about taking a long walk in the park, and later that night, on
the other side of the Parkway, Patti Labelle brought Teena
Marie on stage to sing a duet. Now that was a good day!
That day is only one of many good days with good friends
that this life has blessed me. There are an abundance of days
like those that I reflect upon when clouds roll in to block my
sun to negate all the good life has brought my way.

It is so easy to let the bad out shine the good; that is
why we have to act like vigilantes for the good memories.
While lying in her bed, after a stroke, I remember my Mom-
Mom telling me: "I have had a good life." I remember
wondering how she could think that in her confined state. I
thought about what I knew about her life. She had not
attended college, worked in a prestigious position, or gained
what the world would call riches and fame. However, anyone
who knew her, knew she loved to smile and to laugh. I
remember one time we were at a restaurant and she and I
laughed so hard, I thought I was going to die because I could
not catch my breath. I remember her zest for life and
admiring how she lived life on her terms and did not care
what anyone thought about her. How fulfilling it must be to
feel your life is "good" no matter where you have to get off
its ride.

I know Mom-Mom suffered heartaches and disappointments, but those things did not derail her dreams or define her life. At the end of her life, there were no sad tales or stories of regret. In fact, many times sitting by her bed, we concentrated on all the good God blessed her with like the last man she married at the age of 60 who loved her silly and all those other days in between and after he died.

My friend, Denise told me she has never had a bad day. I am not as confident that I can say the same. Perhaps what she means is that she is able to find some good in every day. The good might be the blessing of waking up. The good might be having another opportunity to find your purpose to earn your space on this here earth. The good might be making someone laugh and to find good where there was none. What is good is personal and relative, but in the end there is no disputing the good that is for you in each day you choose to see it and to embrace it.

Recall those days when you said: "that was a good day; I had a ball!" I now understand that it is the culmination of those days that helped a woman like my Mom-Mom say: "I have had a good life" because it was the good that got her through.

Personal Challenge: It is so easy to remember the bad, so let's bring the good into focus. Think of a good day from your past and from your present. It needs to be a day where just the thought of it makes you smile or laugh out loud. Add colors to your list and detail your good day.

Sight	Smell	Taste	Sound	Touch

Writing Prompt: My Good Day....

Everlasting Life

I cried like a baby when my cat, Princess died. Princess held the secrets of my youth and my dreams. He was the friend in the storms no one ever knew about because they weren't there. He watched silently, without judgment, as I tried on different facades and images trying to figure out me. He was my constant. The one I could depend on to be there regardless if I was fired from yet another job, disillusioned by yet another love or friend. He was a "cool cat" to anyone who had the chance to know him. My then 11-year old daughter, in her wisdom, climbed in my bed that day, put her arm around me and said: "he's not dead because he's still right here," pointing to my heart. In those few words, she had summed up life and death. Somehow she understood that they both are intrinsically connected.

When you lose someone, you lose their earthly presence, not the purpose of their existence. Everything they gave you stays with you. It's hard to see this at the time. I tried to hold onto my cat even while he was in pain. I remember my mother telling me about the guilt she felt when she told her mother it was okay to let go, releasing her from the cancer that plagued her. Part of loving someone means letting go when it is time; there is no guilt in that. This is part of the process of living, being able to love and let go. It almost makes loving seem like a masochistic endeavor. But would you rather choose the alternative and not love at all?

Whether it is a parent, sibling, close friend, or family pet whom you love, part of loving them is being unselfish enough to let them have their peace. Regardless how long they lived, we must understand that they did their job. Their job may have been to just birth you, to raise you, to inspire

119

you, to teach you to love and to trust, to give something unexpected to the world, to challenge you to fight for those who can't fight for themselves, or to show you a window to yourself. Whatever the job may be, the only one with the time clock is God.

I felt silly and apologized about lamenting the death of my cat I had for 19 years, while a friend spoke of the death of his father. His response was: "Loss is loss. There is no big or small." Mechanisms aren't in place to weigh or measure loss; it just is. It is not for us to understand, but to feel. Feel it as deeply as you did the love. Let it rejuvenate you through the memories that resurface from your soul. Part of what makes you sad is wondering if you gave them enough of you while they were here because the totality of what they gave you lies heavily upon your heart when they depart. You begin to remember their subtle idiosyncrasies, things shared in tight corners, bedrooms, kitchen tables, back yards, or corner bars. Here lies the magic of their visit on this plain; all of those moments are what make their lives worthy. It is the good stuff they leave that makes you laugh to yourself in a crowded room. The stuff that saves you because they showed you another way. Wrap yourself in the love stuff they left you, and you'll realize they aren't gone; they are still here in another form.

Personal Challenge: Sometimes our loved ones leave before you have a chance to say goodbye. Take time and list all the things you wanted to tell them while they were still here in this physical realm.

Sight	Smell	Taste	Sound	Touch

Writing Prompt: Dear loving Spirit...

Chapter 8

BE FIERCE

Breaking Glass

There are many forms of glass: stained glass, fiberglass, porcelain, thermoplastics, and more that I do not know to name. What I do know is all are made to be broken or shattered. So when my student told me I was "foolish" to believe glass ceilings were unbreakable because "they" or "the man" will only let you go so far, I was amazed how his logic defied physics. His logic not only defied physics, but also historical evidence.

For over 400 years, our African ancestors, who were enslaved in this country, consistently broke through what appeared as impossible barriers to claim their freedom. They did it beating their drums to incite the Stono Rebellion, they did it when they dared to turn the La Amistad around, and again when David Walker wrote his appeal. They did it when Phillis Wheatley, George Moses Horton, and Harriet E. Wilson penned their way to freedom, and again when that gun-toting Nat Turner, Harriet Tubman, and our Buffalo soldiers blasted their way free. Then there is that other sister named Harriet Jacobs who sat in a cramped garret for seven years with that ceiling crowning her head and bending her spine to spy on her children and biding her time to break free. I wonder if my student would tell Frederick Douglass he was foolish to believe he could break the glass around the books that held his knowledge hostage to trap his body and mind in an enslaved state? Was he then foolish to see through it to defy white supremacist expectations of humanity to travel across continents to establish a newspaper, *The North Star*, to agitate to free his brothers and sisters who were still in bondage while there was still a bounty on his head?

The same glass our ancestors broke is still being shattered today by those folks who decide to dream and to claim what people say is impossible. People may not be a fan of Steve Harvey, but he has no problem telling folks about sleeping in a car because he believed in his dream, and he now has a nationally-syndicated radio show and three television shows. Oprah Winfrey, the product of a single mother, also suffered childhood trauma and is now one of the wealthiest women in the world. There are not many African Americans who were born with silver spoons in their mouths. They all had to blast the glass. Regardless of what you think about what Obama should have done for Black folks, it is because of Barack and Michelle Obama and those who believed that the white glass around the White House was breakable that eight-year old Black boys and girls will never look at that house, built by captured Africans, as one they cannot live in too.

We walk on the shattered remains of glass used to segregate us from offices, hotels, buses, water fountains, bathrooms, and boardrooms. Some families feel the crunch of it beneath their feet when their children defy the school to prison pipeline to sit in a college class room instead of a cell, or to graduate from college instead of being released on probation. I recently told a group of out-of-school and out-of-work 20–24-year olds, who are signed up to take a certificate course to be nursing assistants or home nurse aids through the Department of Employment Services, that these jobs are not their ceiling and that everyone can be Indians, but some of them can become Chiefs and learn the trade well enough to build their own home nursing agencies or go to college to become nurse practitioners or doctors. I wanted them to know that they are just like my students sitting in my

124

college class room who are sitting on centuries of splintered glass left by earth-shakers who understood the privilege and responsibility to go back to pull up the next one who foolishly believes something man made, not God made, is able to cap their dreams. All they ever need is the vision and the will to break the glass.

Personal Challenge: You are already standing on broken glass. Acknowledge the glass breakers in your life and also acknowledge what you have done which you and others did not think you capable. Access the dreams you have for yourself. What are the obstacles you believe inhibit you from becoming or doing the thing you want? Make three columns. On one side list your dream or goal i.e., to complete school, buy a house or become a politician. In the column next to it write what you believe to be the obstacle. In the last column write how you will break the glass.

Sight	Smell	Taste	Sound	Touch

Writing Prompt: I'm breaking the glass

126

Just Dance

People who know me, know I love to dance. They know a party don't owe me nothing. They also know I'm rhythmically challenged.

I remember being eight or nine and my cousins, Tracey, Lukey, and Shirley, forming a circle, clapping their hands and marching in place to teach me to hear the beat. I never forgot that lesson. But the minute I hear my favorite tune or the banging of a drum that sweeps me up in its tempo, the lesson quickly leaves.

Music makes my soul happy, gets my toes to tapping, fingers snapping, and before I know it, I'm in the middle of the floor dancing. I don't care if I get the dance right or if I'm wiggling in time because I'm just doing my dance.

The only time I feel uncomfortable dancing is when I become concerned with what others think. When I begin to concentrate on anything outside of how the music makes me feel, my dance steps falter. I don't move naturally because I'm not listening to me. I'm listening to the critics outside of me. I remember coming off the dance floor years ago, sweating and happy, and this girl I used to go to parties with saying, "you sure can't dance." On another occasion, a girlfriend who rarely partied with me said, "I thought as much as you partied you could dance."

Both times, I was stunned that they had enough time or interest in my dancing to critique me when there was a party going on. Although their comments hurt me, they didn't stop me. They acted like they wanted to snatch back my Black people's card! When Ellen DeGeneres breaks out in dance on her show, she doesn't have to worry about that pressure. She doesn't have to worry about knowing or showing some bad ass move; she just busts-a-move all her own.

Each of us have encountered moments when we have shied away from the dance floor, too afraid to take center stage. Recently, I was tasked to organize and host a reunion of poets who are all part of a seminal anthology. Afraid my steps or my voice would fail me, I stopped myself. Unsure of how my efforts would be perceived, I thought to take the easy exit. Easy exits are not easy; they are fake exits. Fake exits are exits made by people who think they have the power to decide your worth, and you believe them. In the end, it wasn't about worth; it was about planted seeds that were not ready to blossom to do their dance in the wind.

I find I become more self-conscious about my dance moves when I partner with fear. I have to put on headphones, so I don't hear the naysayers who agree with my fear. I have to dance in spite of and sometimes alone to get the job done. There are those times; however, when I am able to shake fear loose. Like when I was in a Paris night club, and they were playing some great music; I was dancing so hard, I didn't realize people had formed a circle around me. I didn't know if this was their version of the soul train line or what? All I knew was I was in the middle of the crowd dancing. It took a minute before I realized they were cheering for me. As soon as I noticed, I froze and I started laughing as I left the circle's middle.

I was laughing because I enjoyed my short visit with that bold, brazen girl who made her way onto the dance floor not giving a damn who was watching or how she looked. The girl some said ain't have no rhythm, who couldn't dance, who needed to isolate her hips more was dancing by herself in the middle of the floor before a crowd of strangers in

Paris! My dancing hushed the naysayers with the clap of my hands, the stomp of my feet, and with the wiggle of my Nana-blessed hips. Not caring how it looked or what other people thought, I did me. I just danced.

Personal Challenge: Today, practice not asking anyone's advice or opinion. Consider only what you think. If you have never gone to a movie alone or restaurant alone, get dressed up and take yourself out on a date. Today be fearless doing YOU!

Sight	Smell	Taste	Sound	Touch

Writing Prompt: What does it look and feel like when you do you? When I do me....

Just Drive

What I remember about the last time I went skiing was that I was too scared to jump off the lift once I got on; so I decided to treat the lift like an amusement park ride and let it take me back down the slope. To my surprise, a return trip was not possible. The only way down was for me to ski down. The one thing I remembered from my ski lessons as a teenager was how to fall in order to cause the least amount of harm. As soon as I looked down at my destination and saw how far I had to go and how many slopes I had to overcome to get down, I got scared and decided to go for the safe fall.

What I hadn't realized was that falling down and getting up at the age of 14 is far easier than when you are 30-something. I could not get up without help, and because I had to sit in the snow so long to get help, I decided falling was not a good idea. Once I returned to an upright position on my skis, I decided just to look ahead, not down, to the side, or backwards just straight ahead. Eyes facing front, I enjoyed the view a little better; my heart didn't race as much, and I didn't get nervous again until I reached my destination and tried another way to stop other than to fall.

The lesson I learned that day sticks with me every time I am faced with a new challenge. Lately, I have found that it is easier to accomplish my tasks when I tell only the people who are needed to help complete the task. I decided to limit the amount of oversight I let others have on my decisions and new directions. Without other folks' opinions or doubts nagging in my ear, I am allowed to look forward. I don't look back at my mistakes or the mistakes of others. I don't take a sideways glance wondering, "what if?" I don't try and guess how long it will take to get to my destination, what slopes I have to overcome to get there, or what the end result might be; I just look straight ahead.

I have been guilty of swooping in on someone's dream for themselves offering my edited version when I had not dreamed nor authored any of it. The bottom line is that no one knows me better than I know myself. That is why I feel guilty when I don't live out my dreams or live up to my God-given talents and gifts because deep inside, I know I took the short cut. We know when we have settled for the safe 9-to-5 route instead of reaching beyond the space of our cubicle. We know when we have squelched that voice that wanted to sing and offer testimony to those who would tell us the road is too tough, and the journey is too long, to realize our dreams so that they, too, would get off the side line of life and get into the game. I personally know that feeling of responsibility to do more with my talents and to continue to stretch myself beyond spaces of comfort to get uncomfortable trying to do something else so that I don't fail myself.

No one likes to fail or to fall, but the truth is we have all done both more times than we can count to get to where we are today. How else would we know what success looks or feels like if we didn't know the fabric of failure. Just drive the bus. That is what my cousin, Tonya, told me when I spoke to her about being conflicted about the next steps I wanted to take in my career.

Recently, I have felt like Jerry McGuire when he boldly sends out his mission statement and then realizes how naked he has left himself to the world. That is how I feel when I boldly push forth, crossing out completed tasks on my "to-do" list. There is trepidation and fear as I move forward, but there is also that sense of accomplishment that I am doing my best and being my best. My nephew, Khalil, said it best, "in the car of life, there is a long road with infinite turns with no maps, signs, or directions…you just drive."

Personal Challenge: Taking a look at what you have on your To-Do-List for the week, how does it partner with the plans you have for the next five to 10 years. Are you in line with your mission? If you look at yourself as a job, what is the mission statement for your corporation called you?

Sight	Smell	Taste	Sound	Touch

Writing Prompt: Think of yourself as a corporation. Provide a name and define your company's mission statement in no less than one paragraph. Ex: My Corps' mission is to . . . . . .

Fearless

During Landmark Forum's Extraordinary Life seminar, I along with the other participants were given the task of listing our fears. The women in my group each spoke about the ways in which fear shows up in their lives. To me, it was as if they were giving life to their fears. I suggested they give life to the many ways they move in the world that are fearless. I challenged them to examine how everyday they walk in their fearlessness.

For instance, there are many ways I challenge what appears as fear. I do not like elevators. I don't know whether I watched too many movies where the bottom fell out or people trapped inside, and that developed my fear. Yet, every day I choose the elevator instead of the steps to get to my office. Every time I stand before my class to give them a lecture, there is a certain amount of fear about how to keep them engaged in what I am trying to teach them. I have no idea what is going on in their life or in their world, which will impact how they receive what I have to give.

There are countless ways fearlessness shows itself. In a conversation with my friend, Sam, she was upset with herself because her fear made her take longer than prudent to address a medical issue. I informed her; she can't beat herself up about the fear, and that she can praise herself for stepping into her fearlessness to get the proper diagnosis to remedy her issue. I also challenged her to see the many ways in which she has always been fearless: becoming a top IBM employee with only a high school education, quitting a six-figure job to pursue her art, going back to school at 50 to complete her degree, publishing a book of poetry, writing a novel, creating a visual art collection to be admired by the world, and designing SOAR's website without prior experience. She has always been fearless.

Being fearless is natural. From your first steps to the first day of school, you step into your fearlessness. Whenever I step into a new venture, I remember my child-self who always believed her dreams would soar and reached for them despite discouraging background noise. My fear was not wrapped up in trying but in not trying. I never wanted to be assailed by what ifs and coulda been, so I did it anyway. My most successful moments and achievements have come when I didn't recall past failures or doubts and just did the damn thing, fearlessly walking into my destiny. Sometimes, I recall the memory of making a blind call to land my first job at the newspaper, writing my first story, leaving there when I feared becoming complacent, having a baby, starting a business, buying a house, going back to school, and so many other events and situations I survived in between to remind myself of being fearlessness. So when I decided it was time to relaunch SOAR and I began to take those first wobbly and unsure steps, I recalled all those times I fearlessly walked into my light. The world could say otherwise, and I didn't care. My relaunch of SOAR was scary, but it was scarier to not listen to my call.

If you live long enough, there are enough things that will happen for you to learn fear. There are enough things to happen in life to make that child in you who was fearless stay tucked underneath the covers of past failures. In this way, you are more like children than children. Children fall down; they cry, and then they try again. Try holding a child back from continuing to play after they fall in a playground, a tantrum will ensue. I assert that your inner child is tucked under the covers. Under the layers of doubt given by

136

naysayers or perceived failures, your fearlessness is still alive in its natural state and waiting on you.

Personal Challenge: Take a look at fears you believe are real and imagined. List five of these fears and decide to challenge yourself to face one fear a week.

Sight	Smell	Taste	Sound	Touch

Writing Prompt: I am fearless….

Chapter 9

LIVING ON PURPOSE

Punk'd

I got Punk'd. No it wasn't by Ashton Kutcher from MTV's show titled "Punk'd" or any other entity. I got punk'd. I let someone take me off my square; move me from a place that I had always known. Since I can remember, I have always been a writer. I have diaries, stories, and poems from as early as seven years old. Yet, after one year of grad school, I considered everything I had written as unworthy. I got punk'd because when push-came-to-shove, I let it shove me over an edge of self-doubt.

When I complained to my little sister Nikki, she said: "Kim, don't let them knock you off your square." Those words, along with zoning out on the MTV Punk'd marathon, crystallized what I was feeling. Then I got mad. I got mad that I had allowed myself to become defeated because someone dared to not fall in love with my keen insight or how I language images.

During my first year of grad school, I was in a constant chase to figure out how to claim that ever elusive 'A.' One day, after receiving another 89 on a paper, I just walked home in the rain with tears of frustration streaming down my face. It seemed I could not rebound. I needed some Jordans, Nikes, or something that could make me jump higher to claim the prize. As a result, I began to think that my acceptance into the program and fellowship was a fluke. Someone had made a mistake and forgot to tell me. I wanted to be the best and brightest but felt I was consistently coming up short. Writing has always been the one thing that propelled me to the front of the class. I wanted my As back. I wanted, needed them to remind me that I was not mediocre, and that my writing was still good and worthy for print.

This feeling of lack is what left me open to being punk'd. I let a grade determine who I was and my worth. If I had not forgotten myself, I would not have felt at times like I wanted to jump off a roof after the second rewrite. I would not have shied away from writing poems, entries in my journals, or beginning new writing projects. If I reminded myself of who I was, a writer; I would not have allowed myself to think differently while learning how to improve my writing. If I had known who I was, no one with a mere slash of a pen could have made me feel less. In truth, no one can make any of us feel, think, or believe anything we do not already believe on some level already.

I was so far off my square that I thought the negative things I was saying to myself were my inspirations to do better. In actuality, all it did was push me further under the covers. Beating up on self does not motivate action; it cripples action. The world has enough ways to beat us up; it can get along well enough without any assistance. Without creating a new system of self-talk, I could not have moved from my bed to my office and then to my computer.

My friend, Tamara was quoted in *Essence* Magazine saying:" you know you are on purpose when you can't think of anything better to do." I got punk'd because I had doubted the purpose God had for me. I forgot what God instructed me to do with my writing and blessings. I got knocked off my square without having anything "better to do." And when I thought about my purpose, I got punk'd back on my square and came from under the covers to write it down.

Personal Challenge: Examine your self-talk. In what ways does your talk negate your worth and purpose? For example: You may say, I'm so stupid; I know I need to leave this job. You may actually think if you talk bad enough about yourself, it will motivate you to act. It will not. The challenge is to change your talk. Instead of calling yourself stupid, say: "I'm going to live on purpose in a new job" or whatever it is you need to do to move you toward your purpose.

Sight	Smell	Taste	Sound	Touch

Writing Prompt: I am on purpose…

Living Life Golden

SOAR was invited to conduct a series of workshops during the Living Life Golden empowerment retreat for women in North Carolina. As SOAR's workshop facilitator, I shared the writing tools needed for the women to access their inner wisdom, and they in turn shared with me their abiding faith and the reminder of what it means to live life golden.

They reminded me that no day is promised. Their stories spoke to me about the necessity of making wise choices. They reminded me that my choices could determine my day and the rest of my life. They reminded me that I have not always made the best choices when it comes to who I have decided to allow in my life or my temple. In order to live my life golden, I have to not let lust or loneliness determine who is allowed to enter my sacred space.

Living my life golden means I act in spirit. Inspiration is not an outer thing; it is an inner communion with the Most High. When I act in spirit, I am able to claim God's promise to give me my hearts' desire, which is in alignment with my purpose. One of the ladies asked me if I had a business card on me. I did not. I have a bad habit of not carrying them with me. My friend, Laini, reminded me that when I worked for other people I carried their cards, so why do I not carry my own? I had to look at that. When I got home, I took a handful of my business cards and put them in my purse. Walking without my cards means I am walking away from God's promise for me. It means I am not walking on purpose. I am not acting in spirit, which means I am not living my life golden.

Living life golden means that I cannot go against the inner voice that guides and protects me. I cannot act like I did not hear it or that it was saying something else just because the task is hard. I am not living my life golden if I live in fear. I must listen. I must put the oxygen mask on me before I give it to others. As a mother and a woman, it is easy to forget this important instruction that is given on every airplane flight. That means that I cannot feel guilty on days where I do absolutely nothing because that is what I was supposed to do—nothing. That is the day to recharge myself to go forward and instead of worrying about doing nothing I need to be still and let my spirit be recharged. That is the day I was gestating to birth a new me.

Just because I am inspired to share what the Creator puts on my heart and it in turn feeds and nurtures others does not mean that I do not still have some work to do. I am clear that I am only the vehicle. In the safe circle that was created during the retreat, I let the women see me just as they showed themselves to me through their writing and sharing. Too often, people are in a hurry to put folks on a pedestal because they speak from a pulpit of their understanding. Pulpits are fragile. People fall. The common denominator is that we are all people. Every day is an opportunity to reassess, revisit, and revise who I was yesterday. It is an opportunity to remind myself to live my life golden. I give thanks for the company of my sisters who revive me and remind me to live my life golden. Life is only hard when I forget.

Personal Challenge: Recognize all the gems in your life. Assign gemstones with your attributes.

Sight	Smell	Taste	Sound	Touch

Writing Prompt: Adding a list of gemstones and using the words in your training wheel write:

My life is_____ because I am.....

Walk the Water

The level of passion a person exhibits in their work tells the difference between a person walking on purpose and one who is not. To walk on purpose sometimes means taking a risk. Risk is the ultimate act of faith, like Jesus asking Peter to walk on water. When someone is pumped up with their God spirit, their skin radiates and their energy does not give way to bitterness, indifference, or regret. They are willing to walk the water on purpose to their dreams.

How do we keep our original dream of ourselves alive amidst life's twists and turns? We are all born with the capability and belief that we can do the thing we were born to do; however, remaining true to the dream takes another type of endurance—the ability to risk. We must use our hips or the balls of our feet to bounce back. We must walk the water of faith even when we seem too old to take the risk. Success does not have a timeline. What we deem as success may not be how the Most High sees it at all. Too often, success is measured by what we see, how much money we make and how visible we are to the world. What is forgotten is that faith is all about walking the water and knowing without seeing that our walk is supported.

Anywhere we choose to look, we can find people happy doing what they are meant to do or people going through the motions, plowing through each day for the purpose of a pay check. We can see it in their eyes and the excitement or hope they are able to translate to others. What really is sad is when we look at them in ways that they have stopped looking at themselves. For if they were still able to see themselves, perhaps it would be enough to revive their energy to crawl out of their safe corners and to try again; the

147

corners they choose to hide in when the thing they tried for seemed too hard or unattainable, so they stopped believing. Instead, they sought a safe place which did not challenge their sanity or livelihood. They killed a bit of their spirit in order to maintain the status quo. See, the real success is when we have the strength to try again. Life can burn us out. It is not always fair. Some people are not nice and will try to hurt us. Some people do not work as hard and do well. Some people will try and hold us back because our star is shining while theirs has forgotten how to glow. Some people do realize the grand dream with what appears like little struggle, but it is all relative. If we really had the opportunity to switch lives with another person, would we do it? Most times we look at the greenery of other folks' lives without smelling or stepping in the manure that made it grow.

Try again. It is all about taking a risk to walk on purpose. In fact, the real risk is in not having the faith to walk the water. Don't be scared. Don't look down. Don't worry about drowning, just walk the water, and walk on purpose.

Personal Challenge: Think about the ambitions you had as a child and how and why they have changed. Think about how you would earn your space on earth if you did not have to worry about money. In fact, make a list of the kind work you would do if money were not a concern.

Sight	Smell	Taste	Sound	Touch

Writing Prompt: My purpose is…

Mid-life Flight Risk

This morning, Toni Morrison's words provided comfort to me. She wrapped me in a blanket of self-renewal when I read the wisdom in her words: "I don't [...] I can't worry about failing now. I don't have another life and I'm not sure how much time I have left in the one I have. I have to take risks and that means that you have to be willing to have it fall like a plate." I had just spoken with my girlfriend, Pam, who gave me the book, *Toni Morrison Conversations*, the night before when I was feeling like I was running out of opportunities and possibilities because of my age. I wanted to know where the bold, self-assured woman who took risks out of necessity sometimes (and fun most times) was hiding. I wanted to know when I decided to go undercover to a safe place where I didn't have to worry about having the fortitude or the guts to rebound from the risks I must take to complete another set of goals.

It is because of my fear of failure that I have always pushed myself to take risks to make things happen. In my youth, I risked embarrassing my family by writing a personal story on abortion which I submitted and was published by *Essence* Magazine. I didn't query my family or the magazine; I just did it. Part of being a writer is the willingness to risk rejection which is what I have done over and over.

Lately, it has taken much more inside talking to gather up my nerves to send my proposals to agents and stories to magazines. I have walked a little wobbly-legged to podiums where I am required to give a speech or to deliver a poem. I ward off my fear by telling myself, "Whatcha going to do, fail?" Or I scare myself with the idea of being the "joke" of the day, which is entirely unacceptable. So I take the risk of making a fool out of myself before crowds because to run is failure and to not do a good job is failure. In my mind, failure is never an option.

I remember a girlfriend prematurely fearing her husband's reaction to his mid-life crisis and telling him when it happens, "just buy the red sports car." I'm not sure if what I'm experiencing is called a mid-life crisis and if it can be fixed with a shiny, new, red sports car. Although, I will admit, I will be happy to give it a try. Really, it just might work because part of my issue is that with the successful completion of a lot of major goals, the only personal experience I have with a brand new car is riding in someone else's brand new car. I also thought by now either my permanent residence or my beach house would be featured in *Interiors* or *LifeStyle*. Instead, I don't have a beach house, and my permanent residence is a good candidate for an Oprah home make-over. Yet, my spirit whispers to me that the attainment of these material trappings will still not make me happy. I probably will find something else to challenge my idea of success. I will find another something undone that challenges what I perceive as a time-limited goal.

Reading Morrison's words turned my thoughts of time and failure on its head. She reversed my whole way of thinking about time in relation to risk and failure. No, I'm not as young as I used to be when I sashayed in and out of adventures trying to find my niche. I don't need to jump in and out of things on a whim anymore. I know who I am and where I fit within the universe. As BOLD as I *thought* I was, nothing is compared to how bold I must be with less time to rebound from the risks I must take.

A buddy of mine told me he thinks, as 50 creeps up on him, his life is just beginning because he has done all the crazy things in his youth. Thinking about the time I have left, I wondered aloud, "beginning?" While I was contemplating the middle and end of my life, he was looking at it as his beginning. He sees it as his beginning because he knows who he is and has a clearer path to see the road he must walk.

Finally, I get it. I get what a wonderful gift he has given himself—the gift of timeless possibility! To think, all the risk taken in youth is to get to a place of endless possibility. The endless possibility comes not with just the willingness to take risks but to acknowledge failure as a possibility that holds no power over what is possible or its outcome. Without the willingness "to have [whatever I try] to fall like a plate" I will suffocate myself with words that never experience air or be like a wingless birds unable to risk the flight.

Personal Challenge: Go and risk letting that thing you have been trying to do or say fall like a plate.

Sight	Smell	Taste	Sound	Touch

Writing Prompt: I'm letting it fall like a plate, and I like the sound…

Chapter 10

STEPPING OUT ON THE EDGES

Remember Your Wisdom

One Sunday afternoon, my lil sister, Nicole convinced Tye and me to visit the Meditation Museum. We were all curious of what could possibly be on display, so we went with Nicole to explore this new space. What I encountered was not a place filled with artifacts to appraise and admire, but a still place where I was able to encounter me. The museum is a place to revisit the wisdom that sometimes escapes me as I walk my path.

While sitting in the quiet room, Spirit blessed me with a few epiphanies. The first was that I do not have to chase what is already mine. Knowing what is already mine means I must learn to surrender, but even more importantly have faith that what God wants for me is already given. The knowing also extends to understanding that I have a right to what I want and deserve the gifts God has promised me.

These gifts are not all material, but some are. At the time, I fretted about how to purchase the car of my dreams. Once I surrendered, things fell in place and within the month of my encounter at the Meditation Museum, I was driving in my dream car. I am blessed to be given the gift to do work I love and to have health insurance. In these days and times, that is surely a gift. I am blessed to be given the gift of love. I have no desire to chase it down. What or who God has for me no one can take away or alter its path.

The other epiphany I had, while sitting cross-legged, staring at a picture of a radiant sun, was how we all are like rays from the sun. Looking at the light streaming from the sun, I began to think of how our individual gifts stretch like tentacles of sun rays with the ability to bring light in the world. For me, my gifts are my words, my facility with language, my oratory skill, and my compassion for others. Those are my rays of light I shine on others. The more I am able to stretch myself, the wider the space or territory increases for me to affect change and to bring light. So with renewed vigor, I remember to be fearless when shining my light. Which brings me to my final epiphany, during my encounter with me: how the soul, powered by God, lets the outside world trick it into fear. Are outsiders more powerful than God? No. Therefore, how does fear exist? It exists when we forget our connection, when we forget the wisdom learned while snapping beans in Grand mom's kitchen, eavesdropping in on grown folks' conversations, or our inner wisdom—known by some as intuition.

I know sometimes I forget my own wisdom. I sit and contemplate life, over analyze outcomes, and pray the fear of the unknown does not overwhelm me. Yet, I do find comfort knowing everything I need to know is right here in me. All I need to do is to have the faith to remember.

Personal Challenge: Intuition is your God voice, the voice of wisdom. Think of one thing you have done lately that might have turned out differently if you had followed your intuition, your God voice; what some call your first mind. Look and discover what voice circumvented your God voice. Why did you not trust your wisdom? Use the following writing prompt as a prayer or mantra to celebrate the wisdom in you.

Sight	Smell	Taste	Sound	Touch

Writing Prompt: Mother, Father God, I am thankful for the Wisdom in me......(begin to list and remember the many ways your wisdom shows up and the ways in which it has and will continue to save you)...

Give Praise Anyway

On my way into church one day, I witnessed one of
the ushers remove three young adults from the sanctuary.
The usher admonished them for laughing at the worshipers
who were caught in the throes of the Holy Spirit. She wanted
them to understand that their laughter was ignorant because
they didn't know what kinds of demons were riding the backs
of these people. They didn't know if they were shouting
words of praise, running down the isles with arms akimbo to
dance off the agony of being raped, the torture of losing a
child, spouse or loved one, the distress of joblessness,
homelessness, or trying not to lose their minds. What she
said to these youth appeared to be as foreign as the culture
they decided to visit. On the other hand, I have never looked
at a person praising God in this same way. So when my
friend asked me what wisdom I could share with her God-
fearing daughter who feels she has done everything in
accordance with the word and is still disappointed with her
outcome, I say give praise anyway.

After the prayers comes the praise. You give praise
anyway. You say thank you Mother/Father God for
blessings seen and unseen. You do a spiritual tap dance for
the blessings that are on the way. My daughter told me she
did the "happy dance" after she received a college acceptance
letter. Yet, how powerful would it have been if she had done
the "dance" for its impending arrival? Praise is a measure of
faith. It's dancing and showing thanks before the blessing
arrives. You shout because you know it's on the way. Praise
is the "blessed assurance." Praise gives you something to do
while you are holding on for the deliverance from your
current situation.

There are some mornings when songs of praise are stuck to my tongue. Songs with words like "I feel no ways tired/ I come too far from where I started from/ Nobody tole me the road would be easy/ I don't believe he's brought me this far to leave me" bring tears to my eyes and revive my faith. I'm thankful God doesn't care if I'm on key or off key, as long as I'm giving praise. When I think of spirituals like this and others that speak to "how I got over," they glorify his "Amazing Grace" and remind me that sometimes "after you've done all you can do, you just stand." My spirit jumps in celebration for all that I have been saved from, delivered from, and have survived. These songs are called spirituals because they are seated in the crest of my soul to give voice to my God spirit that seeks to celebrate the possibility of who I am able to be.

Praise is the cornerstone of faith. Faith is that mighty crane able to lift boulders of financial worry and survival nightmares. Sometimes a bad day can overstay its welcome by weeks or months. During times like these, I remember my father's words: "a bad week doesn't make a life." So when thinking about what wisdom I might share with my friend's daughter, I can say: "I am a witness to how faith works, its ability to let me see the muscle in a new day and to give praise anyway."

Personal Challenge: Look at the situations in your life that appear imperfect, and say thank you. For example, if your loved one disappointed you, say "thank you." Throughout the day, with your whole body and soul say "thank you." I have personally found this good when I am in traffic because the traffic may be keeping me or blocking me from harm. So, just say thank you.

Sight	Smell	Taste	Sound	Touch

Writing Prompt: Mother, Father God I live in praise and thanks for...

Too Busy Being Grateful

I get into these slumps. These pull-your-teeth-out-your-head before you move your butt slumps. It's like super glue holds my feet in place halting all movement. I have analyzed these moments of inertia. At times, it is the fear of the unknown; sometimes it's because I simply do not know, but most of the time it is because my human form is assailed with the flaw of doubt, which makes me believe that I am less than a conqueror of my challenges. At these moments, I am so consumed with what is going wrong that I forget to be grateful.

While waiting for an elevator, I asked an older woman waiting with me "how are you?" She replied: "I'm too busy being grateful to complain." In that moment, she showed me the grace of being grateful. She went on to tell me, she just turned 65 and began touching her toes, twisting her torso, and marching in place to show me that it is by grace that she is able to be so grateful. I applauded her ability because I know people half her age who are not able to give that display of agility. I know some folks who will not even make it to 65 because they do not grace their bodies with the respect needed to show they are grateful to be alive.

I am sure she could have found some stuff to complain about, like I did when I first got up that morning. I had a laundry list of stuff that just wasn't right. I had so much on me that I decided to pray. See prayer is the only way for me when I cannot see a way. It is through prayer that I get my help. I am so grateful that I have prayer to remind me of just how blessed I am. Once I begin praying, I cannot just talk about what I don't have without acknowledging all I do have. I have to first give thanks for waking up, so I am able to give thanks. I have to give thanks for the health and safety of my child, my immediate family, and friends. There is not a place in prayer for me to complain without being grateful for all I have.

I am grateful for a Grand mom who reminds me I must "know Him all the way." I believed I did "know Him;" but if I did "know," like my Grand mom knows, I would know "that a dollar don't make nobody happy." I would know and believe that a way will be made and that all the fuss and stress I am going through is only temporary because in the end, it will be alright. I would know that my belief cannot be arbitrary and that the Most High is not a bank where I can make withdrawals without also making deposits.

Yeah sometimes I wake up in a slump, feeling less than grateful because I'm not focused on my blessings. I feel less than grateful until I take stock of all my limbs that work right, my mind that is able to think right, and my body that is able to sit upright. I am again reminded of the "Grace" that comes with being grateful from my 99-year old Grand mom who knows what "hard times" feel like and continues to be grateful that she lives by Grace. Being grateful is so much easier because if I am too busy being grateful then I don't have time to complain.

Personal Challenge: For a whole month, write down one thing you are grateful for on a slip of paper and put it into your grateful jar. At the end of the month, read and compose a prayer of gratitude.

Sight	Smell	Taste	Sound	Touch

Writing Prompt: I am grateful for…

Prayer Works

While experiencing a particularly challenging situation, I called a friend for consultation and a solution. When Loretta offered to pray with me, I looked at the phone in frustration and told her never mind and that there was a martini somewhere with my name on it. To me, prayer was not a solution. I would rather contemplate my problems while sipping a drink, which is never a solution, only a momentary escape. To me, her solution to pray was a cop-out because she didn't know what else to say. Prayer appeared to be too abstract for such a tangible issue. My problem appeared too large for prayer. I thought I needed something visible to turn the situation around before realizing all I needed was prayer.

When stuff happens, you can get so caught up in the madness of the moment that you only look for answers in man-made solutions. You turn to people for help, hoping they have a recipe that they can pass down to you and to cure what ails you. What I found is that although ailments may appear the same, each ailment has an individual root cause which calls for an individual remedy. What might work for one person will not necessarily work for you.Anyone who has children might know this. Each child is endowed with idiosyncrasies that do not allow you to treat them all the same. What one child might respond to another will not. You have to take that child's personality into consideration before choosing a school, clothing, or a method of correction. Sometimes all you can do is pray.

Besides having a child, prayer is the most revolutionary thing you can do in a time of war. I am not talking about the wars created by punks in power who send other folks to fight the battles their wolf tickets cannot purchase. I am talking about the war in our streets and in our homes against unknown enemies who seek to destroy the moral fiber that makes wrong and right a murky decision. I am talking about outside influences that make prayer an abstract idea because there are so many new advances in technology that are able to provide the answer. With the advance of the Internet, surely if you Google it, the answer will appear online. You can Google prayer, but the one you need is only found when you tap into your private line.

I am always in awe when I hear those praying women dressed in white who circle folks who come to the altar. Their prayers sound like a speech authored for the heavens. They are able to wrap up all the concerns spoken and unspoken. They tap into the need buried in the chests of those too afraid to sing their own complaints. They humble themselves before the Most High, releasing and surrendering all. It is the memory of these praying folks that I called on when the martini did not bring about an escape or solution. I sat in the center of my bed, breathed in God's love for me, exhaled all fear, and then I morphed into the praying women I remembered in my Grand mom's church on the altar who handed over all.

I prayed until tears of understanding streamed down my cheeks. I prayed until I felt lifted up beyond the sanctity of my space into another realm of belonging. I was beamed up into another galaxy where I was humbled and forgiven for forgetting that prayer is all I have ever had to deliver me and to keep me all my life. I gave thanks for all the prayers answered and wondered how I scoffed at the idea of prayer? The moment I believed that prayer was too abstract to work was the moment I felt lost in the madness. I am happy to

165

report that once again my prayers were answered; reminding me prayer works and is the best solution even when I think I know what to do; I will just pray.

Personal Challenge: While listening to your breath during meditation, see what begins to appear before you. Let your breath guide your prayer. Without editing your feelings or visions, write your prayer using the writing prompt below:

Sight	Smell	Taste	Sound	Touch

Writing Prompt: With open heart and mind I pray…

Chapter 11

REMOVE THE LAMPSHADE

Get Your Happy On!

I refuse to be unhappy. I like to smile, laugh, and have fun too much to remain unhappy. I am clear that being happy is a state of mind I decide to have. It is not something someone can gift wrap and bring to me. No one is able to make or control my happy. People have actually asked me "why are you so happy?" I answer with a laugh: "why are you not?"

I detest being unhappy so much that when something upsets me or has my stomach curled in knots, I give myself a time limit to wade in the water of despair. To me, there is nothing worse than being unhappy. Have you ever looked at a person whose face appears to always look like they will cry at any moment or has a consistent snarl? I don't want to show myself to the world that way. I don't want to appear to the world with a face that looks twisted by the fate of my existence. I have seen these people. You don't even want to talk to them because when you do, they make even a "hello" sound like a cuss word. All they see is what is wrong with the world; they even find wrong in being happy.

You cannot make someone get their happy on; they have to want to be happy. Now you can enhance their happiness, but they cannot receive what they do not believe exists. Some folks just don't believe they have earned the right to be happy. They are wrong.

In order to claim your right to be happy, you have to clear the path. You have to clear the path of people who do not honor, respect, or value who you are. You have to understand everyone has a purpose in your life, but it might not be long term. Feeling less will not make you happy, and accepting less will not make the situation or relationship

169

easier to tolerate. I remember asking a girlfriend why she and her partner split up. She said: "he didn't want to be happy." She was clear that she was not responsible for his happiness and that the decision to be happy was one that affected him, not her.

Happiness takes maintenance. In order to maintain my happy, I cannot dwell on past mistakes. Mistakes are missed opportunities to do something different that are only corrected by my present actions. I maintain my happy by not surrounding myself with people who think living with drama is living, and playing the victim is how to become a star. I maintain my happy by realizing there are stages of sadness and to exit stage left when the show is over. I get my happy on when I share a good laugh with a friend. I am happy when I see a sunset full of colors only a painter can describe. I'm happy knowing life is for the living, so why not have a ball!

Personal Challenge: Decide today that yesterday was the last day you were going to dispense energy to a particular dilemma in your life. For instance, after being deceived by a lover who I thought was a friend, I was depressed for weeks. A girlfriend came over and told me that day was the last day to reminisce and be unhappy about that man and that experience. Whether it is losing a job, mate, or money, the pity-party ends today. If someone should ask you about it, say, "all is well."

Sight	Smell	Taste	Sound	Touch

Writing Prompt: All is well......

More than a Slice

Ships at a distance have every man's wish on board. For some they come in with the tide. For others they sail forever on the horizon, never out of sight, never landing until the Watcher turns his eyes away in resignation, his dreams mocked to death by Time. -Zora Neale Hurston

Recently, I was stopped in my tracks when a sister I know said: "I wonder if my daughter and I dream big enough?" I asked her to explain what she meant. She went on to share their dreams and also the fences that confine their dreams from reaching beyond familiar boundaries. She wondered if she dreamed big enough because she was not able to see beyond the parameters of her immediate world, but something in her knew there was more. I am not one to sit in judgment of someone's dream, but I couldn't help but wonder how a dream is able to be small? A small dream appears to be in contradiction to the concept of what it means to dream. Yet, what this sister is saying is less about the size of the dream but more about the imagination and fearlessness it takes to dream about things that are not a part of her reality, about things she did not have a point of reference for or could see.

When I think about the power of dreams and the necessity to have a dream, I think about one of my favorite books, *Their Eyes Were Watching God*. In teaching the book, one of the questions I ask my students is: "what is Janie's dream for herself?" They are stumped. They are stumped partly because some had not completed the reading and partly because they did not think of her in terms of having and ultimately gaining and living her dream. I then ask them about their dreams. Most replied to finish college and to get

172

a good job. Some talked of dreams they've had since they were small. The vast majority could not answer the question. Unlike Janie, in the novel, who dared to step beyond the fence of her grandmother's vision of a good life and walk toward a horizon to birth an empowered self to release her dreams, some of these students' dreams suffered a still birth. It occurred to me some of these students did not know the difference between a dream and a minimum requirement for living.

Dreams are not about limitations; they defy limitations. They defy limitations because they are fearless. They believe the impossible is possible. There is a saying, "if you can see it, you can be it." Perhaps all you need is some Windex, so you can see beyond your current reflection to visualize the self you are able to dream into being. It means having faith that you deserve every good thing, and it is there waiting for you to claim. What are you scared of anyway? It doesn't cost a thing to dream; dreaming is free. Dreams only become nightmares when you avoid their existence or lack the courage to make them a reality. Dreams become nightmares when you realize life is a banquet and you choose to starve to death. Imagine the nightmare of getting to the end of this thing called life to find out all you had to do for things to turn out different was to dream different.

Some folks think if they just ask for a slice of pie instead of the whole thing they have a better chance at getting a little taste, and they will not appear greedy. I say get greedy. Get your eat on! Have a greedy dream that gives you the whole dang pie! Why settle for a little bit? God got greedy when she made this huge world. She got greedy with the shades of colors she wanted to see on people, animals, insects, and the sky. She got greedy with the variety of humans, their shapes, forms, and imaginations. She dreamt this whole thing up in seven days and gave us minds to help along her vision. How dare I or you fall short on her dream? She showed us the power and purpose of a dream, so we could know its possibility. If you wonder if you are dreaming big enough that is God whispering in your ear that you are not dreaming at all because you have not tapped into the power of your imagination. Just look at the dream of her apricot, plum, magenta, or teal-colored skies to see she has already showed you how—now eat the dang pie!

Personal Challenge: Create a Vision Board. To do this you simply need magazines, scissors, glue, and cardboard. Cut out pictures that show where you are and where you want to be. Also cut out words to affirm the vision you have for yourself. Images and words have power, so be selective. Add what you write in your prompt to your board.

Sight	Smell	Taste	Sound	Touch

Writing Prompt: My dream _____ is bigger than me

Shine With Your Brilliance

As I sat watching American Idol one night with my daughter, a young woman waiting to audition spoke about her fear of singing in the lead because her comfort zone was singing back-up. I don't remember the song she sang although I rewound and played it back twice. I played it back because this woman who felt comfortable in the background had one of the most brilliant voices the judges or I had ever heard since the beginning of the show. I played it back to see if she was authentic in her expression of utter disbelief that they thought she was *that* good. I sat there and cried because I soon realized she did not know or believe in her talent, and that her lack of belief and fear were the components that held the power to kill her chances. For some reason, this woman had become comfortable with the lampshade that hid her brilliance.

After watching the show, my daughter asked me why I was crying? I told her because I could not figure out how someone has that kind of talent and keeps it in the background. I then grabbed her and reminded her of what my mother has always told her: "shine with your brilliance." I wanted to remind her of the many great qualities she has and to not let anyone interpret her greatness. I wanted her to remember her voice and to not let anyone usurp what she has to say. I wanted to make sure I said these things because I know, regardless of what I say, there will be someone out there that might make her feel unsure. Because they are unsure of their own gifts, they will try and rob my baby of hers, so I have to put in as many safeguards as possible.

The truth is, regardless of how much I say she is brilliant, she must internalize it for herself. I know because I

176

still struggle with it. I cannot count how many times I have asked God if writing is what I am supposed to do and to give me a sign. Each time he answers. He answers through various awards I have earned and publications. Yet, when stuff gets hard, I go back and ask, "Now, are you really sure God?" The bottom line is I have to believe. My girlfriend, Sam, always tells me, "Nobody can say what you have to say the way you say it." These words act as my reminder as I face the editors of my work and professors who try to convince me I am not good enough. I am enough for me. Just as you are enough for you. You can always improve, but at the end of the day when you have done your best, you are enough. You are brilliant.

There is a line in Zora Neale Hurston's *Jonah's Gourd Vine*, which comes up for me: "God don't call no man, [...] and turn im loose tuh fool." In other words, God put a gift in you, a light to shine on the world, not to squander and to become too paralyzed by fear to use. The fact that you are here means you have been called to do something on this planet.

I wonder what happened to the American Idol contestant to make her comfortable in the background? American Idol is only the vehicle God used to push her out of her comfort zone to take the lampshade off her light. You must listen to the calling and know God has your back. You cannot play your life small when God made you in the image of greatness. Let God's light beam within you and shine with your brilliance.

Personal Challenge: Look back in your come from place, and the genesis of your fears will surface and only then will you understand how to annihilate the false evidence which appears as real.

Sight	Smell	Taste	Sound	Touch

Writing Prompt: Under my lampshade I see …

Brave Enough

Being "brave enough" is the crux of what I need to be. I cannot sugar-coat or find another way to say it, and believe me I have tried. I cannot dismiss that Spirit has whispered instructions in my ear of what to do to move forward and I did not act. I did not move on the ideas given to me because I allowed outside opinions to impact how I moved, when the "idea" was not given to them. I am clear that it is me that allows someone else to have power over my actions, not because they are right but because I am not brave enough to act on the instructions given to me.

Being brave is not a small feat, which is why some heroes earn medals. You don't always see yourself as brave because when you think of heroes you think of people who have survived wars with valor or you visualize super hero forms able to stop bullets or to spin webs over their enemies. True bravery is applicable to everyday life. Not giving up is brave. Having a double mastectomy to ward off impending cancer because you realize your breasts are not you is brave. Taking an HIV test and living your life to the fullest regardless of the results is brave. Testing out a dream no one else believes in is brave. Getting up and putting one foot before the other even when you don't know your direction, but you keep stepping anyway is brave. The ability to step past the fear and step up for you is brave.

Stepping up for you may mean revising the resume and sending it out not as a preemptive strike but because Spirit has said it is time to move. Stepping up for you may mean being brave enough to face the anger or the hurt rather than taking something to numb the anger or to numb the hurt. Stepping up for you may mean being brave enough to

179

look at your relationships to evaluate whether or not you are getting what you want. Being brave enough in relationships is hard because you are forever putting your heart on the line when you open it to others, trusting they won't run from what keeps your heart beating.

Remember going to the amusement park and looking up at the biggest rollercoaster in the park? Do you remember summoning up the courage to give it a try and when you were finally brave enough to get on the ride, you had immediate misgivings once the latch on the seat was secured? How about when the ride finally started up that first hill, and the anticipation of the impending fall made you look back and scream for someone to let you off; and no matter how much you cussed and screamed as you endured one coaster dip after another, your only recourse was to hold on and to stay in your seat to survive the ride. What you realize after going through the bevy of mixed emotions is that you did survive, and most of the times you were even brave enough to get on another ride.

Personal Challenge: Life is like an amusement park with a variety of rides for you to try. Today, list three things Spirit has told you to try and then be brave enough to go for the ride.

Sight	Smell	Taste	Sound	Touch

Writing Prompt: Today I face the Lion in me and roar with my possibility to ....

Chapter 12

LOVING UP ON YOU!

Caught Slippin'

I was slippin'. Not on a wet floor or on an unseen substance in the street. I was slippin' and slidin' on me. I was even slippin' on the words needed to express what was happening inside of me. I let folks get away with laying their garbage at my door. Yeah, I was slippin' on other folks stuff until a friend caught me and saved me from cracking my head and busting my butt on some crap that was not mine.

At one point, I thought I had a sign on my head that said, "all crazy people stop here." I had to ask myself why I let them in and entertain them once they arrived. I thought I could handle being a receptacle for their pain, childhood disappointments, and unresolved anger. I thought I could insulate myself from harm. Words do hurt; even if you know what someone says is not true and that their words say more about them than you. They still hurt. I don't care how balanced you think you are, being the target of another person's abuse knocks you off balance. I began to wonder if I was crazy for trying to investigate the catalyst of their dysfunction. I thought I could then show them what their crap looks like when they throw it at another person. The problem with that strategy is that unlike a broken arm, you can't fix crazy.

Everything and everyone does not need nor want me to fix them, some just want to be let go. Although I don't like to give up on people, especially family, I have learned everyone is not able to appreciate my light and love. I remember again Mrs. Pouge saying: "you can't throw away family." Well, I may not throw them away, but I can provide enough distance to reevaluate how and when we might share the same space. Then there are some folks that pass through with too much toxic waste for me to ever consider sharing the same space.

When I start slippin' on me that means I need to cleanse my space. A fast is a perfect way to stop myself long enough to gain clarity. When I cleanse, I detoxify my system of waste. I am able to see what crap is mine and what crap is someone else's. I wobble under the weight of excess crap. I cleanse so I am able to see what is versus what I want it to be. I have learned in relationships that if you have to work too hard for that person to gain an understanding of you, then more than likely there is an attraction without a connection. A connection is something you feel, not something you force. If the feeling does not flow in a mutual direction, you have to let it go. You cannot divert your course from your wants and needs to make the unworkable work.

So when my dear friend told me I was slippin,' I took it as a wakeup call. I needed to check myself and the invitation cards I was sending out. No one can spend more time in my space than I allow. I had to own my part and empower myself to be okay with cutting folks off and letting them go to preserve the core of me. Preserving me means being good to me, which means I'm not caught slippin' on someone else's crap.

Personal Challenge: Where in your life have you been caught slipping—a time when you were out of integrity with yourself? To be out of integrity is not bad or good, but it might be uncomfortable. Think about the wisdom that has been shared with you this week. Meditate on the best of you and the ways the best of you are not being shared. How do you get back to you? Separate the laundry of issues that are yours from the stuff others have loaded in your basket. Make a list of the things that weight you down. People often project onto others what they can't deal with about themselves. They shuck their responsibility and make you deal with it by placing the blame on you. Recognize all the things that you know are good and worthy and begin a list. After your list is complete, put the training wheels together and claim your space on the page.

Sight	Smell	Taste	Sound	Touch

Writing Prompt: I almost slipped on this...... and it ain't mine.

The Give Back

What a great gift to know who you are. To know yourself so well you don't compromise on what you want or need. To some, this is known as being selfish. My friend Sam and I discussed this notion at length. Sam proposes that selfishness has been given a bad rap and that to some extent the most loving thing you can do is to be selfish. It might be a matter of semantics because being selfish does not necessarily have to mean you disregard others in order to regard the self. Ultimately, when you are being selfish, you are doing something to make the self feel good, and that is not a bad thing. It is a very self-loving thing to do. For you can't give others the love you don't have.

For instance, when you give to charities or to a loved one or others in need, what appears as a selfless act is indeed selfish? It is selfish because of what giving gives you back. Giving to someone might give you back a sense of accomplishment, joy, self-satisfaction, or self-redemption. Even when an action appears to be about someone else, in the end, it is about how the action makes you feel about yourself. If you did not feel good, you would not do it. Who purposely does things to make themselves feel bad?

Being selfish also means you must sacrifice the need to please other people. I am an old movie fan, and a few of my favorite actresses are Bette Davis, Katharine Hepburn, and Joan Crawford. In their auto-biographies they talk about themselves as women who turn deaf ears to what other people think or societal norms but listen to their own desires, not at the expense of others but in spite of others. They act selfishly to obtain their goals. What is most impressive is that they are unapologetic. I also have great respect for my great-grandmother. She told me one day that she was unapologetically mean and selfish. She hated sharing my great-grandfather's affection with her eight children. Even though I agreed with her, I tried to dissuade her from this belief. She did not want absolution; she wanted to be understood. She knew who she was and was fine with it, and this I respect.

Selfish is not necessarily a bad thing but a necessary thing. I have a dear friend who wasn't selfish enough with her time and energy and now, after a double mastectomy, she is forced into selfishly loving herself into wellness. I have a student who thinks it's better to miss a class than to disappoint a friend. When we know our priorities, we know what is necessary to do to meet them. I remember while I was writing my thesis, I could not attend my friend's father's funeral and how bad I felt because I needed to be selfish with my time to meet my deadline. Joe understood. He, more than anyone, knew that my non-attendance did not mean I did not love him or want to console him but that I needed to finish what I started.

Life is filled with distractions and selfish moments. In the end, it is your choice how selfish you decide to be in order to receive "the give back" that loving yourself promises.

Personal Challenge: Look at where you have been selfless and where you have been considered selfish. Are the selfless places filled with obligations for others that drain on you and go unnoticed? Are the times when you are considered selfish times where you did something for yourself without consultation or agreement? Which act is costing more energy? Think of selfish in a new way. Look at it as an energy saver; a way to replenish the self. Take a warm bath with rosemary and lavender oils. Close your eyes, listen to your breath, and meditate. Once your meditation is complete, use the writing prompt below:

Sight	Smell	Taste	Sound	Touch

Writing Prompt: I restore the spirit of Me …..

Get it Right

I woke up one morning feeling like nothing goes right for me. As I let this thought slide down my spirit and out my mouth, I knew I was wrong. Yet, its pull was strong. I thought about all the things I tried to do that had not turned out "right." I was on the proverbial roof ready to jump when I heard Tamela Mann's song on the radio, "God Provides." One of the verses says something about even if I don't have a place to sleep or food to eat, God provides. That stopped me cold. What kind of faith did I have to let me sink into an abyss of disbelief? I instantly felt ungrateful, selfish and wrong. To get more clarity, I called a sister-friend I've named as my Touchstone. I told Sam about how I was feeling and how the song touched my soul. Once I detailed to her the four things I thought were not "right" with my life, I began to contradict myself.

My house, my pay, my child, and my love life were to me not in their "right" order. I had not made the right contractor choices for my home, which consequently has stalled its renovation. Although I now have three degrees, my pay is disrespectful. I have nurtured and helped several students claim their college degrees, but I have been unable to make sure my own daughter secured hers in a timely manner. As for a mate, I deserve so much more than the men who show up in my life. All of these claims have some validity but also are able to be contradicted.

I may have been duped by contractors, but I have learned some very expensive lessons that will result in a house beyond what I had first dreamed or envisioned. No, I don't make the right pay, but no one can pay me what I'm worth which motivated me to relaunch SOAR. It also does not mean I am not in the right position as a teacher for many of my students. I was sure of this when one of my Middle Eastern students cried in my arms after disclosing to me that he was dyslexic. I knew his passion for learning did not match his efforts, so I requested a meeting with him. After a little prodding, he detailed a long history of learning challenges that he had overcome and wanted to prove to his parents he could learn like anyone else and did not need a special school. I shared with him how I understood his shame because I have a learning difference too. It took me years to admit this, and I still work hard to not feel less because of it. In fact, most people who learn differently are usually very intelligent because they overcompensate to hide their difference. It is this sensitivity that I bring to my classroom and students, which is why I try multiple teaching strategies for as many students to "get it" their individual way.

As for my not choosing my "right mate," my sugar-blood Angel and I wondered if there was a man we missed. When we went down our independent list, we both acknowledged we didn't miss the "right" man. Whoever "he" might be, he has not ducked or dodged us, nor have we ducked him. God knows better than us what kind of preparation "he" needs and the things we need to do solo without the distraction of a mate who is not right for us. What I know for sure is that who God has for us will be there for us. Anything not right, God will remove.

As for my daughter, graduating in four years is not always in the plan. It wasn't for me. It took me almost 20 years before I completed all of my education. I did not and do not want her to experience the same time-frame, but sometimes it takes that long to figure out your passion and to be in the right position when opportunities make themselves available. I can

190

truthfully say, I don't feel behind any of my peers who graduated decades before me. In most cases, we are in the same position of revisiting and reclaiming new careers. As an educator, I felt I had a special key to ensure my daughter's success. However, what I did do right was raise a young woman I can say I like inside and out without hesitation. She is funny, smart, fair, talented, and wise. She is my "go to person" and the one able to "get me right" when she hears me saying the wrong thing about myself or others. I could not have birthed a more "right" soul who has now birthed my most perfect blessing, my grandson, Cairo. Further, if God chose me to be her mother, I must be some kind of "right" in the world.

Sam and I went back and forth contradicting my "right" analysis. She told me how I talked her off the roof many times and helped her to get out of her head and out of her own way. And because of that, I was the "right" friend for her. Listening to her, I became more ashamed that I even let these thoughts nestle themselves around my center or soak up time in my spirit.

I am no different than anyone else who wishes things worked out differently or as planned. What I didn't plan and what I am most grateful for is my "right" village. I have friends in my village who in most cases are closer to me and know me better than my family. I cherish them as much as my family members who show up for me. God has provided me a "right" village who encourages and keeps me steady on my right path. To say anything different is to say God got it wrong.

Personal Challenge: My son-in-law has a favorite saying: "there's nothing missing and nothing broken." This has been a difficult challenge for me when thinking about my unfinished home. The gift in the challenge is stretching yourself to see yourself and your circumstances in a new way. When you consider something or someone not broken then you are able to see what is right.

Sight	Smell	Taste	Sound	Touch

Writing Prompt: I'm good with me…

Belong To You

Anyone who knows me knows that two of my favorite books, *Their Eyes Were Watching God* and *Sula*, are written by my favorite authors, Zora Neale Hurston and Toni Morrison, respectively. These women set me on the path of understanding what it means to "belong" to you. When you belong to yourself, you understand that love is not ownership and that the self does not come in dissectible parts. You are complete and whole unto yourself. What some may call your flaws and imperfections, you simply see as idiosyncrasies.

When you belong to you, the necessity of belonging to someone else is unimportant. You don't want to lay claim to another person because you do not want anyone to lay claim to you. You find that the thing that complicates most relationships is the inextricable need to claim someone as your own, as if they came into this world for you. They did not. They came into this world to do some work and to share some of the love they have with the other souls they bump into along the way. No one is the exclusive domain of another. Once you try to box in the love, or the person, you begin to choke off some of their air and your air as well. You can't breathe right, worrying about phone calls, dates, chocolate-covered candies, and trinkets because you confuse "belonging" with what society has made you think are protocols of belonging to another person instead of being alright with belonging to you.

The joy of belonging to you is that how you respond to another person comes from a well of love inside you that allows you to treat others as kindly as you treat yourself. You don't need outside demands to instruct you how to act because you know how to act with you, and the person

193

sharing your space is but an extension of the love you choose to shower on you.

There is a freedom that comes to you when you really understand this concept. This freedom does not mean that you are irresponsible with the feelings of others, but what it does mean is that you own the freedom to love you and others on your terms. There is a freedom in understanding that love is not an outside thing but something that must reside and grow from the inside. It is not something you can grab from someone else.

More importantly, you can't give yourself away thinking someone else will find you and bring you back to you. One of Momma Emma's favorite sayings is "you don't come in body parts. They got to take the whole person." Sacrificing parts of you to gain attention or love robs you and the other person of the full experience of you. Belonging to you means that you feel free enough to show up with you, not as a dare but as a gift that does not lose its value if it is not accepted by another person. You are free to move about this world tasting everything like it's new because you are open to how life unfolds daily.

Belonging to you means you take responsibility for it all. You are responsible for how you decide to love, to learn, to work, and to move in this world. The blame game is gone. One of my favorite lines from *Sula* is when she says, "I don't want to make somebody else. I want to make myself." She understands she is the creator of her universe and she is responsible for how it is shaped. Just as Hurston's Janie understands her love for Teacake is not a result of belonging to him but of having the freedom to belong to herself. Once you understand and revel in the knowingness of belonging to yourself, you will never claim another person as yours

194

because you will be having far too much fun exploring and belonging to you.

Personal Challenge: Think about the ways in which you challenge others expectations because you are being true to yourself. Additionally, think of the ways others inhibit your need to think and to be different in the world and the constraints you might put on others because of how you were taught people should perform in certain relationships. Once you have given this some thought and jotted down some notes answer the prompt.

Sight	Smell	Taste	Sound	Touch

Writing Prompt: Dear Universe….I belong to the spirit of me who….

The Best Me

Recently, I gave my freshman students the task of writing a paper to discuss their best self. I thought it was an easy descriptive essay, but they were perplexed. They started asking me: "are you talking about the best me in the future or what is my best thing?" I told them, they were making the essay a lot harder than it needed to be and that they needed to relax and to think of ways they show up now as their best self. I told them I would join them in this writing assignment. Once I began writing, I realized that the question I had asked of them was a trick question because the best me is an evolutionary endeavor.

I remember telling someone that I had written my best poem. He laughed at me while saying that it was impossible. I thought he was being dismissive until he asked me "how could that poem be your best when you are still writing poems?" He was right. Since that conversation, I have written several poems that I have considered my best. I don't even remember the poem I originally thought was my best poem because my writing has evolved to other levels.

As I thought about the best of me, I thought about my daughter and the feeling of not recognizing my own beauty until I looked into her face. It was easy for me to see my best reflected back at me in that moment. It made me wonder about how many of life's speed bumps I would have missed if I had recognized the best of me before I gave birth to my daughter.

In many ways, getting to my best is about giving birth to new selves. I am consistently surprised by my ability to inspire a crowd or a classroom full of students. It is my responsibility to leave people who come to hear me speak or my students with some good food. I am able to birth a new self when I ask the Most High to use me as the vessel it needs to speak through to change a mind or to uplift a spirit. It is an out of body experience that I welcome. I not only enrich others, but I learn something new too. I am introduced to a new possibility of who I can be in the world and with that there is a responsibility to not be less.

There are times the best of who I am does not show itself. When my ego blinds my intent and my purpose is no longer clear, then my ego has deterred me from being my best self. When I'm cut off in traffic or someone is going 25 mph when the speed limit is 55, I am definitely not my best self. When I let jealousy or envy take up residence in my spirit and to show itself through snarky comments, I am not my best self. It is during these times, I know I still have work to do. What is most important is that I am down for doing the work.

My best is an oratory masterpiece; I deliver like a cup of chamomile tea. It is me inspiring others to dig for the more inside them so they can see the brilliance I see sparkling in their eyes like uncut diamonds. I marvel at their greatness some cloak in wild hair, over-sized clothes, stammered speech and behind dark shades. I pour the best of me into them to realize the beauty in their words and in their genius.

When I am my most authentic self, I am giving my best. When I pen myself butt naked on the page, I am my best self. Sometimes I recall that bodacious young woman in her 20s who was told she had "presence." Not knowing what that meant until a decade or so later, I embrace it and always endeavor to show that best part of myself. I am excited by the evolution of which I have yet to become and the best of me that I will show.

Personal Challenge: Think of 10 ways you have improved yourself to reach your personal best in the last 10 years and then think of 10 ways you have surpassed what you believed to be your best.

Sight	Smell	Taste	Sound	Touch

Writing Prompt: The World has yet to see the Best of ME…

Chapter 13

FROM HERE ON OUT

TAKE A BATH

Monday's are known to be blah days, but this particular Monday made me recall the feeling I had when I titled my first book: *Slightly off Center*. I was irritated and off balance. I spoke to my friend Lisa who made me pull up my big girl panties to confront one irritant while she volunteered to take care of another one to lighten my load. Although my sister-friend had rode in for the rescue, I still ended up missing two buses, two trains, paying more for a train ticket then needed and having to call an Uber to get to work on time. I was exasperated, and so beyond frustrated that I collapsed inside the seat of my Uber ride. Resting my head on the back of the seat with my legs stretched out sideways, I heard the Uber driver softly say "breathe." I must admit I was a little spooked, and I wondered if she was talking to me. She had on a music station that played nothing but smooth tunes. I then heard her say, "listen to your breath." I thought I hopped a ride into the twilight zone. I can't tell you how I began to tell her about my morning; but it was part of the release I needed.

I told her that it wasn't one thing that had me feeling off kilter. If I was honest, I was able to trace the feeling back to the beginning of the weekend when I decided I didn't want to join my friends at happy hour. I had decided it was too cold, and I was too tired. This had never stopped me before. On Saturday, my lil sister Nicole and I planned to go see a funny movie. I was looking forward to this because I thought laughter would surely shake and move the cloud hoovering over me. We went to see the movie Fist Fight, and it was the stupid comedy I needed to make me laugh. We then snuck into another movie to see Get Out which I had already seen, but thought it would be fun to see again and to hear the people talking back to the screen. Although I had a good time, something lingered. Sunday the feeling was back, so I decided to shut down except for a couple necessary check in phone calls.

In search of what was wrong, I looked back over my week which included the My Daughter's Power Circle meeting and how good they felt to release their stories and pent up emotions. It wasn't until I thought about the Circle and the things shared that it hit me. For the past month, in my role as workshop facilitator, I had become the receptacle for other folks stuff. I had even had a one on one session with one of the counselors, a week earlier, before I met with My Daughters because I could see she was off her game. After our talk, one of the strategies I gave her to help her move forward was to burn sage in her home to cleanse it of any unwanted energy and to take a cleansing bath of lavender and rosemary. I told her to make sure she didn't put the loose rosemary in the tub like I did which caused a laughable mess. When I saw her the next week, she was back to her bouncy, happy self, telling me she felt renewed.

It had only been two weeks since I gave her that advice, and somehow I had forgotten when it came to my own wellness. It was not only the young women, for whom I was present, but my sister-friends and students as well. I had months of stuff that needed to be released in the water, for me to walk in the world clean.

There is a reason my mother always told me showers are good, but I needed to sit my butt in a bath tub and soak. She has a Sunday ritual of creating a serene space for her weekly soak. This was particularly necessary when she worked as a Victims' Witness Advocate for the U.S. Attorneys' Office. The only way she could stomach hearing the stories of children killed, women raped and families murdered was to take her weekly bath. She took these same social work skills to Namibia where she worked with a group of visually impaired women in the Peace Corps. The only difference was her apartment didn't come with a tub, so she had to stuff her body in a plastic wash tub to maintain her necessary weekly ritual. No wonder she was so excited about the large bathroom and luxurious bathtub we had in one of our rooms when I came to visit her. Knowing the cleansing power of water to release the day, the week or a month worth of other people's stuff, she soaked it all off to emerge renewed.

Hearing the calm and soothing voice of my Uber driver, I was curious about her other occupation. She told me she was a Dialysis nurse. She then told me how drained she feels on somedays when she encounters a particularly challenging patient. In fact, talking to me made her remember she needed to go to a particular store that carries white sage. She burns this in her house to release all negative energy. She went on to give me steps to replenish myself, so I am able to let go of the energy that is resting on my body and in my spirit. She suggested I get pink crystal salt and put it near the door or any crystal salt will do; clean the house with ammonia and put a little in my bath water. The latter she had to admit she hadn't tried, but if I do, to just put in a little and shower. I told her I think I will wash the tub with ammonia and fill it with my lavender and rosemary. She thought that was a good idea, and she added if you don't have any of that, still, just take a bath.

I wrote a poem once about "troublin' the water with lavender and rosemary." So glad I remembered what I already knew to rise from the water clean.

Stay Inspired

While working at the Atlanta Journal Constitution as a copy carrier, I moseyed into the columnist Celestine Sibley's office. I was curious about how she was able to come up with a new column of homespun wisdom every week. I can still see her wizened face wrinkled with years of knowing and giving me a no nonsense stern look when I asked her how she is inspired to write her weekly column. I guess I was expecting some grandmotherly, sweet as apple pie words of wisdom, so when she said, "Inspiration? Damn an inspiration. I gotta job to do!" I was shocked. She gave me an off the cuff candor that has stayed lodged in my memory for the last 30 years. Feeling discouraged, overwhelmed, second guessing decisions and ready to throw it all in like a towel, her words surfaced in my conscious memory.

Her words reverberated in my ears even after I thought about going home to take a bath and perhaps to meditate. I didn't have time for that. I wanted something quick, so I wouldn't lose the momentum I needed for my business or lose hope in the completion of my unfinished home. I was on a downward spiral. It wasn't just one thing that was not going as planned; it was everything. It was as if my mind had decided to make a beef stew of misery by throwing in a variety of perceived problems to replace the carrots, celery, potatoes and green peas. I knew I didn't want to eat it, so I tried to find a new recipe for inspiration.

Ironically, Mrs. Sibley's words were the only thing I could lean on for the inspiration I lacked. Therefore, I decided to learn a little about her life as a reporter, mother and columnist. I learned she was hired as a weekend cub reporter at age 15 and hired full-time by the Mobile Press Register upon graduation. I learned she let others deceive themselves with her folksy stories about log cabins, tea time and Key lime pies enough to surprise them with her moxie and to refuse an invitation by President Jimmy Carter who she felt insulted her. I learned she wrote over 10,000 columns and numerous books to support her family because she loved it and not to get rich. I learned that a month before she died, her impending death inspired her last column. She didn't like to be fawned over and didn't think of herself as a legend because she was just doing the work that had to be done.

It was being able to read over the canvas of this woman's life knowing I will never know just how deep some of the craters she stepped in and walked out of that I used as inspiration. I now understand why she gave me a look that bordered on wondering if I was crazy but knowing I was young and needed a quick lesson in perseverance. She knew most times inspiration wasn't a thing gained from the outside in a book or from Sunday morning praise. It was an ongoing enterprise built from work put in that built steps of endurance. It was the everydayness of a life well lived and getting work done in spite of ole man death perched on the side of the bed with hands ready to snatch the "kivvers."

When I give my own life the same cursory read that I gave hers, I become my own inspiration. I am nowhere near where I began this life or where some forecasted I might be. I only get discouraged when I forget my own story. When I skim the pages of my own experience and don't honor those dark and tight spaces where I thought I would not recover, I miss my opportunity to be inspired.

What I know is that I have been here before. I have been in an uncomfortable place and wondered if it was ever going to change. What I am feeling is not new. In fact, I have survived circumstances like this and worse many times before because I was inspired by my history of resilience and creativity. I cannot let myself get fooled by my present circumstance or get diverted by what I see to the left or right of me. When I read and not skim my own pages, I am inspired by that little girl from Philly who was determined to leave 52nd St to go to college to become a reporter like Brenda Starr and poet like

Sonia Sanchez and who became so much more than what she was able to dream. When I think about her, I stay inspired.

Claim Your Space

It was Gloria Wade Gayles, during my Junior year at Spelman College, who first instructed me to: "claim my space." I in turn incorporated her words in my classroom instruction and in my SOAR workshops. I let my students know that if they do not claim their space, someone will claim it for them. This lesson that was taught to me that I now teach to others is all the more relevant in the climate women find themselves. Lately, I have been pulled into social media battles which illuminate how we use our differences as women to cause a state of distraction. At a time when there is a war to claim our rights to our bodies and our lives, there are women who still struggle with how to see and how to protect other women.

This struggle and divisiveness is home grown. I can't count the times I've heard women say, "I don't trust females;" or "I don't have any female friends." The first problem with these types of comments is the use of the word "female" which can be anything from a female cat to a female roach. The second problem is that the woman, in fact, is saying she doesn't trust herself, and she is not a good friend. Some women grow up hearing and mimic these negative comments expressed by their mothers or other older women who were also taught early not to trust women. Women seldom see how some of this language and behavior is instigated by men who need women to be separate to keep them from knowing their collective power. I remember hearing guys boast about women fighting over them in the street. I also have seen how this fight extends to the workplace. TV shows like Mary Jane display a vivid scenario of this struggle through the older broadcast journalist stepping on the neck of the younger woman for fear of losing her place of power as if they cannot claim a dual space to speak back to power structures that erect glass ceilings to deny them. In both scenarios, the women have bought into a fear of lack: a lack of men and a lack of opportunity.

Neither scenario allows for the women to harness their power or to use their collective wisdom to create a workable space.

Their unworkable space is given language when they describe one another as a "bitch." This word is used by men and women to describe women. Now, some women are torn by whether it is a term of endearment or an insult. As a lover of words, I never thought it was cute or could get comfortable being called a female dog. There was a time when the word was considered a curse word that you would not hear on T.V. Presently, this word that defames women is as common as apple pie. No wonder, one of my students disagreed with me on this point so much that she chose to write an argumentative essay on why it was okay to call her girlfriends "bitches." Her main point: "like dogs, my girls are loyal." Why not call each other: sister, queen or princess? These words fall naturally off my lips in a way "bitch" never will. That's a word that automatically makes the mouth snarl, not smile. Words reflect how we see ourselves and our space in it.

This reflection of ourselves is skewed by the distraction of unreal reality shows where women get paid to degrade and to fight one another and by feminists/womanists arguments that become so lofty they forget the bulk of the women they claim to support. This is why SOAR's My Daughter's Power Circle is so important to me. It is my chance to debunk the negative images that have young women hating themselves and hating other women. It's my opportunity to dismantle the notion of women not supporting women by creating a space where they give each other choice when they believe they are choice-less.

It is my opportunity to take what I learned in the academy and to make it work in the streets. I can either stay on social media debating who is allowed to claim a woman's space because of gender or race differences, or I can go to the women and strategize with them how to galvanize us into action. I don't want the young women I know to be 30, 40 or 50 years old before they realize the strength of their sister's hug. Not long ago, a friend hosted a party for me to gather funny date stories from sisters. We talked and laughed into the wee hours of the morning. A few of the sisters commented they had never felt that level of camaraderie nor laughed that long and loud with a group of sisters. This was at once sad and good to me. Sad because like many sisters, they had fallen for the okey doke believing sisters can't be friends or have fun without a man or men being present. It was good because once they experienced the possibility of sisterhood, and the beauty of themselves reflected back at them in the faces of their sisters, they will no longer believe the lie.

We must first begin to be aware and to be conscious of being a woman who wants and needs to be in relationship with other women. That starts with us. Our canvas is large. I realize I've been blessed with a mother who taught me how to be a sister to other sisters, with the sisterhood I experienced at Spelman, through my associations with the Black Woman's Project in Atlanta, my Spelman Sister Dazon's organization Sisterlove and various female centered groups. The necessity and the power in claiming a space for myself is the necessary space I know we need to claim for ourselves. It can be at lunch with another sister, empowerment seminars, SOAR Sister Circles or any way we decide which does not involve crippling another sister. Not every sister will fall into the fold. I know that; however, I extend what I know about sisterhood because I know it will be her who will hold the cup of my tears.

FROM HERE ON OUT

Remember to Be Good to YOU!!

Notes

Acknowledgements:

This book could not have been written without the wisdom of my grandmothers, my mom-mom, grandfather and other elders who have shared their wisdom with me. My mother and father who always encourage me and from day one have opened the world up to me and for me. My daughter Kali who keeps me grounded and confident that I will leave the world better having birthed her. My niece Jada who makes me remember to laugh at myself. I give a special shout out to my lil sister Nicole Creecy for carving out time to edit this book and to my Touchstones: Sam, Cherne and Trula and my other sister friends: Denise, Loretta, Pam, Laini, Colie, Tye, Nelly, and Lisa who hold the cup of my tears and a bucket full of my joy. My cousins Tracey and Lorraine for being   avid readers and supporters of my Wednesday Wisdom before Facebook; Muhsinah and Janice for sharing my Wisdom with the First Sunday Family, my Uncle Amos who has been pushing me to write another book and a host of other family and friends some of who have also lent their Wisdom to these essays and the others who keep me lifted in prayer and support my wildest dreams. I thank you all including Chris Gumbs, who sat with me all those years ago on a quiet beach in Anquilla where we shared words of wisdom that he told me to write down. I did, and the Wednesday Wisdom column was born.

About the Author

Kimberly A. Collins is the Founder of SOAR (So Others Ascend Righteously), where she facilitates Writing for Healing Workshops and composes her weekly blog Wednesday Wisdom (www.dcsoar.com) Ms. Collins has one collection of Poetry, *Slightly off Center, and* a forthcoming collection of poetry, *Bessie's Resurrection* which is a composite of her study at Howard University (MA) and Spalding University (MFA). She is an English Instructor at Morgan State University. Her most recent poetry appears in: *Revise the Psalm: The Gwendolyn Brooks Anthology; Pittsburg Review; Syracuse Cultural Workers' 2017 Women Artist Datebook; Truth Feasting, Berkeley Review, Black Magnolia Literary Magazine, Black Poets of the Deep South, In The Tradition: An Anthology of Young African American Writers; The Nubian Gallery, NOBO Journal of African American Dialogue, Theorizing Black Feminism, Fingernails Across the Blackboard.* Scholarly publications and magazines: *The New Sound: A Journal of Interdisciplinary Art and Literature, Post- Colonial Composition Pedagogy: Using the cultures of Marginalized Students to Teach Writing, The Dictionary of Literary Biography Contemporary Black British Writers, Catalyst* and *Essence* Magazine.

45042503R00124

Made in the USA
Middletown, DE
23 June 2017